BARBARIAN IN THE GARDEN

BARBARIAN IN THE GARDEN

Zbigniew Herbert

*Translated from the Polish
by Michael March & Jarosław Anders*

A Harvest/HBJ Book
HARCOURT BRACE JOVANOVICH, PUBLISHERS
San Diego   New York   London

First published in 1962 by Czytelnik, Warsaw
First published in Great Britain in 1985 by Carcanet Press Limited
Earlier versions of these essays have appeared in Antaeus, London
Magazine and PN Review.

Library of Congress Cataloging-in-Publication Data
Herbert, Zbigniew.
 Barbarian in the garden.
 Translation of: Barbarzyńca w ogrodzie.
 "A Harvest/HBJ book."
 1. Europe—Civilization—Addresses, essays,
lectures. I. Title.
CB203.H455   1986   940   86-300
ISBN 0-15-610681-7 (Harvest/HBJ : pbk.)

Printed in the United States of America
First Harvest/HBJ edition 1986
A B C D E F G H I J

CONTENTS

ACKNOWLEDGEMENTS

I have fought with the beast. I wish to thank Adam Czerniawski and Piotr Sommer for their help; Lech Jeczmyk for his copy; my editor, Robyn Marsack, a fine editor; the former Polish Writers' Union for the summer of 1981; and Zbigniew Herbert for his trust.

Michael March
London, January 1985

LASCAUX

Si Altamira est la capitale de l'art pariétal
Lascaux en est Versailles.

HENRI BREUIL

LASCAUX is not on any map. It does not exist, at least not in the same sense as London or Radom. One had to enquire at the Musée de l'homme in Paris to learn its location.

I went in early spring. The Vézère Valley was rising in its fresh, unfinished green. Fragments of landscape seen through the bus window resembled canvases by Bissière. A texture of tender green.

Montignac. A village without interest, save a plaque commemorating a worthy midwife: '*Ici vécut Madame Marie Martel — sage-femme — officier d'Academie. Sa vie . . . c'était faire du bien. Sa joie . . . accomplir son devoir.*' Expressed most delicately.

Breakfast in a small restaurant, but what a breakfast! An omelette with truffles. Truffles belong to the world history of human folly, hence to the history of art. So a word about truffles.

They are an underground mushroom preying on the roots of other plants. To uncover them you need dogs or pigs, conspicuous, as everyone knows, for their perfect sense of smell. A certain fly also signals the presence of this gastronomic treasure.

Truffles fetched a high price on the market so the local peasants were overcome by a real truffle fever. The soil was burrowed, the woods ravaged; the trees now stand plaintively dead. Large areas of cultivable land became barren because the mushroom produced a poisonous substance. Besides, it was very capricious and more difficult to domesticate than the ordinary mushroom. With all this, an omelette with truffles is delicious and their smell, as the dish has no taste, is incomparable. Just like the poet Tuwim's mignonette.

One leaves Montignac by a motorway that rises, winds, enters a forest and suddenly ends. A parking lot. A stand with Coca Cola and colour postcards. Those who are not satisfied with the reproductions are led into a yard, and then into a concrete cellar resembling a military bunker. A heavy door is locked, and for a moment we stand in darkness awaiting the initiation. Finally, the door leads inside. We are in the cave.

The cold electric light is hideous, so we can only imagine the Lascaux cave when the living light of torches and cressets set into motion the herds of bulls, bison and deer on the walls and vault. In addition, the guide's voice stammering explanations. A sergeant reading the Holy Scriptures.

The colours: black, brown, ochre, vermilion crimson, mallow and limestone white. Their vitality and freshness surpassing Renaissance frescoes. The colours of earth, blood and ash.

Images of animals, mostly in profile, are caught in motion drawn with both an expansive vigour and the tenderness of Modigliani's reclining women. The images appear chaotic, as though painted hastily by a frenetic genius using cinematic techniques, with close and long-range shots. At the same time they present a coherent, panoramic composition which seems to disobey all rules. They vary from a few centimetres to more than five metres. One finds palimpsests: in short, a classical disorder which simultaneously conveys an impression of perfect harmony.

The first room, called the room of the bulls, has a beautiful natural vault, as though constructed from frozen clouds. Ten metres wide, thirty metres long, it can hold a hundred people. The Lascaux zoo opens with the image of a bicorn. This fantastic creature has a mighty body, a short neck, and a small head with two immense, straight horns. Its small head resembles a rhinoceros, yet it is unlike any living or fossil animal. Its mysterious presence forewarns that we shall not view an atlas of natural history but a region of ritual and magic. Historians agree that the Lascaux cave was not a place of habitation but a sanctuary, the underground Sistine Chapel of our forefathers.

The Vézère River curves among limestone hills covered by forest. At its lower reaches, just before it flows into the Dordogne, a large number of caves inhabited by Palaeolithic man were discovered. His skeleton, found in Cro-Magnon, resembles contemporary man's. The Cro-Magnon probably originated in Asia; his progression towards Europe started after the last glaciation some thirty or forty thousand years before Christ. He pitilessly exterminated the less advanced Neanderthal, usurping his caves and hunting grounds. Man was born under the star of Cain.

Southern France and northern Spain were the territories where the new conqueror, *Homo sapiens*, created a civilization later called the Franco-Cantabrian culture. It developed in the early Palaeolithic, also named the 'reindeer' era. From the mid-Palaeolithic the environment of Lascaux became a real Promised Land, flowing not so much with milk and mead as with the hot blood of animals. Like cities that later grew near the trade routes, the stone-age settlements were founded on the tracks of migrating animals. Every spring, herds of reindeer, wild horses, cows, bulls, bison and rhinoceri crossed this territory to the green pastures of the Auvergne. The mysterious regularity and the blessed lack of memory in the animals, who yearly followed the same trail to certain death, was as miraculous for Palaeolithic man as the Nile floods for the Egyptians.

A powerful supplication for the eternal preservation of the natural order can be read from the walls of Lascaux. That is probably why the cave painters are the greatest animal artists in history. Unlike the Dutch masters, an animal for them was not an element in a tame landscape in pastoral Arcadia; they saw it in a flash, in dramatic flight, alive but marked for death. Their eye did not contemplate the object but fettered it in its outline with the precision of the perfect murderer.

The first room was probably the site of hunting rituals. (They came here with stone cressets for their guttural rites.) It takes its name from four huge bulls, the largest being more than five metres long; these magnificent animals dominate a herd of horse-shapes and fragile deer. Their stampede blasts the cave; condensed, the harsh breathing in their inflated nostrils.

The room leads into a blind, narrow corridor. '*L'heureux désordre des figures*' reigns. Red cows, small childish horses and bucks dance disarranged in all directions. A horse on its back, his hooves stretched towards the limestone sky, gives evidence of a pursuit still practised by primitive hunting tribes: animals are driven with fire and loud noise towards a high cliff and topple to their deaths.

One of the most beautiful animal portraits in history is called the 'Chinese Horse'. The name does not signify its race: it is a homage to the perfection of the drawing of the Lascaux master. A soft black contour, at once distinct and vanishing, both contains and shapes the body's mass. A short mane, like that of a circus horse, impetuous, with thundering hooves. Ochre does not fill the body; the belly and legs are white.

I realize that all descriptions, all inventories are useless in the presence of this masterpiece, which displays such a blinding, obvious unity. Only poetry and fairy-tales possess the power of instant creation. One should say, 'Once upon a time, there was a beautiful horse from Lascaux.'

How to reconcile this refined art with the brutal practices of the prehistoric hunters? How to consent to the arrows piercing the flesh of an animal, an imaginary murder committed by the artist?

Before the revolution, hunting tribes from Siberia lived in conditions similar to those of the 'reindeer' era. Lot-Falck in *Les rites de chasse chez les peuples sibériens* writes: 'A hunter treated an animal as a creature at least equal to himself. Noting that an animal must hunt, like himself, in order to live, man thought that it had the same model of social organization. Man's superiority was manifest in the field of technology through his use of tools. In the sphere of magic, the animal was attributed with equal powers. Its physical strength, swiftness and perfected senses gave the animal a superiority highly praised by hunters. In the spiritual realm animals were credited with even greater virtues — a closer contact with the divine and with the forces of nature, which they embodied.' So far, we understand. The abyss of palaeo-psychology begins with the bond between the killer and his victim: 'The death of the animal depends, to some extent, on the animal itself; it must consent to be killed by entering into a relationship with its murderer. That is why the hunter cares for the animal and tries to establish a close union. If the reindeer does not love its hunter, it will not bow to its death.' Thus, our original sin and power are hypocritical. Only insatiable, murderous love explains the charm of the Lascaux bestiary.

To the right of the room of the bulls, a narrow cat-like corridor leads to the nave or apse. On the left wall a large black cow catches our attention with its perfect outline, and two mysterious yet distinct signs placed under its hooves. These are not the only signs before which we stand helpless.

The meaning of the arrows piercing the animals is clear since 'killing the image' was practised by medieval witches, frequently performed in Renaissance courts and preserved until our rational times. But what are those quadrangles with a colourful chess-board pattern under the hooves of the black cow? L'abbé Breuil, the pope of pre-historians, saw signs of hunting clans, a remote heraldry. Perhaps they were models of animal traps or designs of shacks. For Raymond Vaufrey, they were painted leather coats, similar to those still to be found in Rhodesia. Though these assumptions are plausible, none is certain. Also, we are unable to interpret other simple signs: dots, dashes, squares and circles, and the geometric figures found in caves such as Castillo in Spain. Some scholars timidly suppose that these were the first attempts at writing. Yet only the obvious images speak to us. Amidst the raucous breathing of the Lascaux animals, the geometric signs are silent; and perhaps will remain silent for ever. Our knowledge about our ancestors is modulated by a violent cry and a deadly hush.

On the left side of the nave, there is a beautiful frieze of deer. The artist has depicted only the heads, necks and antlers; they flow like a river towards the hunters hidden in the bush.

A composition which trivializes the violence of our contemporary masters: two soot-black bison with their rumps turned to each other. The one on the left displays raw flesh through a torn patch of skin. Heads raised, front hooves thrusting. The painting explodes with a dark, blind power. Even Goya's bullfights are but a vague echo of this passion.

The apse leads us towards a falling aperture, called a shaft, to a meeting with the ultimate mystery. It is a scene, and as becomes an ancient drama, acted by a limited number of protagonists: a bison pierced by a javelin, a man lying on the ground, a bird and the faded contour of a departing rhinoceros. The bison is seen in profile, but its head is turned towards the spectator. Intestines spill from its gut. A man, his image simplified, has a bird's head with a straight beak, four-fingered hands, spread arms and legs. The bird, as though cut from cardboard, is placed on a stick of straight line. The entire image is drawn with a thick, black line and filled with only the golden ochre of the background. It is distinguished by a raw, almost clumsy facture treatment. It attracts the historian's attention not so much on artistic grounds, as for its iconographic expressiveness.

Almost all Franco-Cantabrian art is non-narrative. Though we know some statuettes and imprints of human faces, man is virtually absent from Palaeolithic painting. Yet, to present a hunting scene one must introduce man's image.

L'abbé Breuil viewed the scene in the shaft as a plaque commemorating a hunting fatality. The bison has killed the man, but the

11

animal's lethal wound was probably caused by the rhinoceros who joined the fight rather than by the javelin thrown at its back. Perhaps the immense stomach wound was produced by a simple stone-catapult whose vague outline protrudes under the animal's legs. For Breuil the stylized bird without legs or beak resembled the burial monuments of the Alaskan Eskimos.

This is not the sole exegesis. The shaft scene has given play to profuse speculation. Kirchner, a German anthropologist, proposed that the scene did not depict hunting: the man on the ground was not a victim, but a shaman in ecstasy. Breuil's interpretation did not account for the presence of the bird (the analogy to the Eskimo burial totems seemed unconvincing) and the bird-shaped head of the prostrate man. These elements became the focus of Kirchner's theory, which referred to the analogy between the civilization of the hunting tribes in Siberia and recalled the ritual of cow sacrifice described by Sieroszewski in his work on the Yakuts. During this ritual three totems were erected and crowned with figures resembling the bird from Lascaux. The Yakuts usually performed these rites in the presence of a shaman who often fell into a trance. His role was to deliver the soul of the sacrificed animal to heaven. After an ecstatic dance, he collapsed as though dead; this necessitated an assisting bird spirit in whose nature the shaman participated with feather dressing and bird mask.

Kirchner's hypothesis is impressive, but it does not explain the presence of the peacefully withdrawing rhinoceros which un-doubtedly belongs to the scene.

Yet another reason for this scene's importance: it is one of the first representations of man in Palaeolithic art. What a striking difference between human and animal form. The bison is suggestive and specific; one can feel not only the substance of its flesh, but also the pathos of its agony. The small figure of man affords the barest of signs: a protracted, rectangular trunk with sticks for limbs. It is as though the Aurignacian painter were ashamed of his body, longing for his forsaken animal family. Lascaux is the apotheosis of those creatures which evolution left in their immutable form.

Man destroyed the order of nature by his thought and labour. He craved a new discipline through a sequence of self-imposed pro-hibitions. He was ashamed of his face, a visible sign of difference. He often wore masks, animal masks, as if trying to appease his own treason. When he wanted to appear graceful and strong, he became a beast. He returned to his origins lovingly submerged in the warm womb of nature.

In the Aurignacian epoch the images of men have the forms of hybrids with the heads of birds, apes and deer: in the cave of Trois Frères a human figure is dressed in animal hide and antlers, presiding as 'god of the cave' or 'the wizard' with large, fascinating eyes. One of the most beautiful portrayals depicts a fabulous animal carnival. A crowd of horses, bucks, bison and a dancing man with a bison's head who plays a musical instrument.

The idea of an absolute, mimetic animal representation, inseparable from the picture's magic function, was probably the reason for the ancient painters' use of pigments. The ancient palette is simple and can be reduced to red and its derivatives, black and white. It seems that prehistoric man was unresponsive to other colours, like the Bantu tribe today. Anyway, the old scriptures of humanity, Veda, Avesta, the Old Testament, the poems of Homer, are faithful to this limited perception of colour.

There was a great demand for ochre. Prehistoric stores were found in the caves of Les Roches and Les Eyzies with traces of larger quarries in the Tertiary Sounds near Nantron. Pigments were formed from minerals: manganese was the base of black; ferrous oxides the base of red. Minerals were ground to powder on stone plates or animal bones like the buffalo shoulder-blades found in Pair-non-Pair. The colouring powder was stored in hollow bones or small sacks suspended from belts similar to those used by the Bushman artists before their extinction by the Boers. Pulverized pigment was mixed with animal grease, marrow or water. Contours were drawn with a stone point; and the paint was applied by finger, fur-brush or twigs. Sometimes it was blown through a special pipe: perhaps the technique used in Lascaux where large surfaces were covered by a coat of uneven colours. These procedures gave the effect of soft outlines and a grainy surface, like an organic structure.

The surprisingly skilful painting and drawing techniques of the Aurignacian, Solutrean and Magdalenian periods has led to the speculation that art schools existed. This seems corroborated by the development of Palaeolithic art from the simple outlines in the caves of Castillo to the masterpieces of Altamira and Lascaux.

The chronology of Palaeolithic art is difficult to determine though more reliable dating may be based on the evolution of tools. In this thin span of human history (thin only for us through the lack of written materials and the small number of remains in comparison to the vastness of the epoch) the clocks measure neither hours nor centuries but tens of millennia.

The early Palaeolithic, the era of reindeer and thinking man, lasted some fifteen to twenty-five thousand years, terminating in the fifteenth millennium before Christ. It is divided into three periods: Aurignacian, Solutrean and Magdalenian. The climate stabilized giving birth to the Franco-Cantabrian civilization. The nightmare of glacial devastation vanished. Yet warmth brought about the culture's defeat: by the end of the Magdalenian era, the reindeer had migrated to the north. Man remained alone, deserted by the gods and animals.

What is the place of Lascaux in prehistory? We know that the cave was not decorated at a stroke and that it contains palimpsests from different millennia. Based on an analysis of style, Breuil decided that the main paintings were made in the Aurignacian period. Their chief characteristic was perspective, though not a convergent perspective based on geometry but rather a 'twisted perspective'. Animals were usually presented in profile while parts of their bodies — heads, ears and legs — were turned towards the spectator. The bison's horns in the scene from the shaft have the shape of a slanting lyre.*

The story of the discovery. September 1940. France has fallen to the Germans. The Battle of Britain is approaching its climax. In the margin of events, a forest near Montignac lends a scene from a novel for adolescents, an adventure which gave the world one of its greatest finds. No one knows when a storm overturned a tree uncovering the hole which excited the imagination of eighteen-year-old Marcel Ravidat and his companions. The boys thought that it was the entrance to an underground passage that led to the ruins of a nearby castle. Journalists created a dog which discovered Lascaux after falling into a ditch. It is more probable that Ravidat had the soul of an explorer, though he cared less for fame than for treasure.

The hole was eighty centimetres wide and seemed as deep. But a stone thrown into it took an unusually long time to reach the bottom. The boys enlarged the entrance. Ravidat was the first to

---

* There is another method of dating archaeological finds. It is based on the measurement of the C14 isotope contained in plant and animal fossils. The analysis of carbon found in the Lascaux caves made it possible to date the origin of the wall paintings to thirteen thousand years B.C. Archaeologists, however, move the date back several millennia.

enter the cave. Someone brought a lamp. And the paintings buried underground for twenty thousand years were revealed to human eyes. 'Our joy was unbounded. We performed a wild war dance.' Fortunately the youths did not explore the caves. They called their teacher, M. Laval; he in turn summoned Breuil who lived in the vicinity and arrived nine days later. The academic world learned of the discovery five years afterwards, at the end of the war.

The boys deserve, if not a monument, at least a plaque no smaller than the midwife's. Their home-town Montignac became famous. And fame brought substantial profits. The town received an improved bus connection, numerous cafés appropriately named 'The Bull', 'The Bison', 'The Quaternary' flourished, and more than twenty families now live on souvenirs. Perhaps Ravidat has opened a restaurant and as an old man will tell the story of his discovery to the tourists around the fireplace; or he will graduate in archaeology. It is improbable that he will ever accomplish anything equally conspicuous. To tell the truth, no one has heard of him since.

Less than a kilometre from the cave, a private enterprise in prehistory was established. The owners of a nearby meadow discovered something that resembled an entrance to another cave and found some trivial fossils. They built a hut to contain these 'items'; and in order to make it appear scholarly, decorated the walls with charts from which one can learn that there were four glaciations: Günz, Mindel, Riss and Würm. A shrewd peasant, smelling of sheep-cheese, is ready to contribute further information on palaeontology for one franc.

Because we live in doubting times, the authenticity of the cave paintings was questioned. We begin with the discovery in Altamira by Marcellino de Sautuola in 1879. The Jesuits were suspected of forging the paintings in order to discredit the claims of the archaeologists, who threatened to extend man's knowledge beyond biblical interpretation. It took scientists twenty years to establish the authenticity of Altamira.

Their scepticism is quite understandable if we recall the famous affair of the Piltdown skull, over which the most prominent archaeologists pondered for twenty years until it was proclaimed a forgery. A forgery unique and perfect as it was prepared by someone who had access to collections of similar finds and the secrets of the laboratory. The processes which can be applied to a piece of bone to render it 'Palaeolithic' are much simpler than painting enormous cave surfaces. The latter requires a team possessing both knowledge and extraordinary artistic talent. An endeavour utterly disproportionate to all profit.

What provokes most suspicion is that some reproductions, including those published soon after the discovery, differ in detail from the paintings to be seen in the grottoes. It is suspected that some effects were added. In magazine reproductions of the shaft scene, the prostrate man has no phallus. This fragment was simply obliterated by editors mindful of their readers' moral sensibility. Since many Palaeolithic statuettes and etchings are connected with fertility rites which emphasize large genitalia, the whole affair becomes clear.

While visiting the Lascaux caves, I myself felt sceptical about the astonishing freshness of colour and the perfect condition of the relics. But the explanation is simple. For thousands of years the caves were covered by earth so they remained in stable physical conditions. The humidity produced a translucent coat of salt that preserved the painted surfaces like varnish.

In the summer of 1952, while visiting the caves of Pech-Merle, the poet André Breton decided to solve the problem of authenticity by a simple experiment. He scratched a painting and, seeing that colour came away on his finger, resolved that the work was a recent forgery. He was fined for scratching though he remained convinced; the affair was not finished. The Société des Gens de Lettres called for an investigation of the painted caves. L'abbé Breuil regarded this request as inadmissable in his report to the high commission for historical monuments. The method of scratching did not enrich the arsenal of archaeological research.

I returned from Lascaux by the same road I arrived. Though I had stared into the 'abyss' of history, I did not emerge from an alien world. Never before had I felt a stronger or more reassuring conviction: I am a citizen of the earth, an inheritor not only of the Greeks and Romans but of almost the whole of infinity.

This is precisely human pride and confession, cast against the vastness of the heavens, space and time: 'Poor bodies that perish without a trace, let humanity be nothingness to you; feeble hands excavate the earth with a trace of the Aurignacian half-beast and a trace of vanished kingdoms; images, though evoking indifference or understanding, equally testify to your dignity. No greatness can be separated from its support. The rest are compliant creatures and thoughtless worms.'

The road opened to the Greek temples and the Gothic cathedrals. I walked towards them feeling the warm touch of the Lascaux painter on my palm.

AMONG THE DORIANS

*The only harmony that gives spirit a perfect tranquillity is the
harmony of the Dorians.*

ARISTOTLE

I TRIED to convince Naples of the artistic merits of
silence. In vain. Some aesthetics are based on noise. So I used an
argument of terror: 'Listen, Naples, Vesuvius never sleeps. If a
tremor should foretell disaster, no one would hear it. Remember
Pompeii's fate. Of course, I cannot demand that you imitate its grave
peace. Yet I long for Pericles' moderation. I say this name not
without reason. For you border Magna Graecia.'

There were only two relatively quiet places: the Museo Capo di
Monte and the lift at the *Albergo Fiore*. The museum is situated in a
large park above the town — its murmur resonating like the voice of
an old record.

I gazed most frequently at Mantegna's portrait of young Francesco
Gonzaga. The boy is dressed in a pink *lucco* and cap, which tries to
cover his evenly cropped locks. Maturity and adolescence contend
for possession of his face. A sharp eye, a strong masculine nose and a
childish, swollen mouth. The background is a magnificent deep
green, alluring, like water under a bridge.

The lift at the *Albergo Fiore* is a work of art. Spacious as a bourgeois
sitting-room with intricate golden ornaments, mirror and settee
upholstered in red plush. The room rises slowly, sighing all the way
for the nineteenth century.

I stayed at the *Albergo* both for patriotic reasons (the owner was a
compatriot) and ulterior motives (it was cheap). Signor Kowalczyk
had fair hair and an open Slav face. At night we talked over wine
about the terrible fates of war, the vices of Italians, the merits of the
Poles, and pasta's influence on the soul. When I confessed my dream
of visiting Sicily, Signor Kowalczyk reached into his desk and

benevolently handed me a ticket to Paestum which had been left by a tourist.

Paestum is not Syracuse, but it is still Magna Graecia. Without much regret I abandoned the possibility of visiting the Blue Grotto. I knew Capri, that 'Island of Lovers', quite well from a charming pre-war song; and I did not want to spoil my rapture by its reality. As it turned out, Paestum would have been worth the pilgrimage even by foot.

The Sunday train reaches Paestum almost empty. Most tourists get off between Sorrento and Salerno where they are greeted by small donkey-carts decorated with flowers. From the station you follow a straight, cypress-lined road to the Gate of Mermaids, where you enter a town inhabited by high grass and stone.

The Greek colonies in Italy were by no means peaceful oases. The mighty wall, in places seven metres thick, offers immediate evidence. From their stony, unyielding ground the Greeks crossed 'the wine-dark sea' to a country warmed by the fires of many generations. The ancient necropolises which date back to Palaeolithic times attest to their fate.

The greatest period of colonization occurred between the eighth and sixth centuries B.C. It was purely economic in scope, thus differing from the previous wave of Greek expansion which reached the coasts of Asia Minor some centuries earlier and had a political basis — namely the arrival of the Dorians from the north.

The first Greek conquests were chaotic looting raids. Legends soon followed, claiming the lands before the first settlers arrived. While Homer shied away from the mythical territories west of the Ionian Sea, poets were busy populating the alien rivers, sea-coasts, caves and islands with Greek deities, mermaids and heroes.

The desecrator Odysseus was not a colonizer but a representative of the mythical epoch. On his return from Troy when he destroyed the Ciconians at Ismarus, he was only interested in shipworthy spoils — female slaves and treasure. No exotic charms could hinder his homeward voyage. The poetry of Hesiod clearly shows that the songs of wandering poets were often substitutes for travel for the landowners during this period.

Sometimes the phenomenon of colonization was rooted in personal causes: a family quarrel or contested inheritance. One should not reject explanations which underlie social transformations: the loosening of the strong tribal bonds prevalent during the time of the

Trojan expedition. Thucydides and Plato give another interpretation that is both simple and convincing: lack of land. Sicily and the lands south of the Apennine Peninsula posed tempting prospects for agrarian and mercantile colonization.

However, these lands were not uninhabited. The Greeks reclaimed these barbarian sites by sleight of hand or by force, with less cruelty than the Romans (those Prussians of the ancient world), though not without bloodshed. They were primarily concerned in securing coasts for their ports. Local populations sought shelter in the mountains, and with hatred observed the growth of opulent towns. Cicero described the coastline as an ornamental band sown on to the rough cloth of barbarian lands, a golden band which was frequently stained with blood.

Poseidonia (Paestum in Latin) was founded in the middle of the seventh century B.C. by the Dorians who had been expelled from Sybaris by the Achaeans. The Greek settlements in Italy fought for hegemony as ruthlessly as in Greece itself. Attempts were made to unify southern Italy through a league of towns. This idea, as can be guessed from excavated coins, was furthered by the Pythagoreans from Croton. The wreckage of Sybaris with its one hundred thousand inhabitants is their work. The alliance of the Poseidonians with the victors was highly rewarded. Their wealth came from trade in corn and oil. Soon ten temples graced the town.

The temples were not just manifestations of a religious spirit or the celebrated Greek love of beauty. Art, especially architecture, played an important role in the colonies by emphasizing Greek ideals. A Greek temple on a hill appeared as a banner hoisted over a conquered land.

Greek civilization reached its zenith during the Periclean period in the sixth and fifth centuries B.C. The merchant towns became the havens of scholars, poets and philosophers who gained considerable political influence. Both Croton and Metapontum were ruled by the Pythagoreans. Those who have read Plato's *Republic* should not be surprised by the rebellion in 450 B.C. against the philosophers who used the worship of numbers as a pretext for ordering the compulsory registration of men, and celebrated the occasion with the imprisonment of all those suspected of anti-Pythagorean sentiments. An ordinary citizen becomes impatient with refined abstraction; he prefers dull, bureaucratic corruption.

Not far from Paestum is Elea, home of Parmenides' philosophical school founded at the turn of the sixth century B.C. It succeeded the Ionian school as the second important link in Greek thought. Pre-classical Greek philosophy came from the colonies.

Perhaps it is naïve, though not unconvincing, to claim that the perpetual state of danger in the Greek *polis* caused the Eleans to preach the consolatory doctrine of the immutability of the world. Though the stilled Eleatic arrow of Zeno was not confirmed by history.

Poseidonia was captured in 400 B.C. by the Lucanians from the surrounding mountains. Seventy years later, they were slaughtered by King Alexander of Epirus, the nephew of Alexander the Great, in a gesture of Hellenistic solidarity. After his death, the Lucanians regained control. Their occupation must have been brutal as even Greek speech was forbidden.

The new liberators were the Romans with whom the Greeks could easily consort. Paestum became a Roman colony supplying Rome with ships and crews. When the Republic was troubled (after the battle of Cannae), the Poseidonians offered golden urns from their temples. The Romans graciously refused and rewarded the colony with the privilege of minting its own coin.

Finally Poseidon, Paestum's patron, admonished his worshippers by raising the coastline. The local river, Silarus, lost its outlet and decayed in the marshlands. Strabo complains about the bad air in the neighbourhood. What the barbarians had been unable to exact was achieved by malaria.

In the Middle Ages Paestum had become a caricature of itself, inhabited by a small Christian community in houses built of ancient rubble clinging to the old temple of Demeter, transformed into a church. In the eleventh century the decimated, feverish dwellers yielded to the pressure of the Saracens, fleeing eastward over the same path taken by the Lucanians in their escape from the Greeks.

In Capaccio Vecchio, where the Poseidonians found shelter, a church was erected dedicated to the Madonna of the Pomegranate. The Madonna has the face of Hera. In May and August the in-habitants form a solemn procession carrying to the church little barges decorated with flowers and candles, which resemble the Greek offerings to Hera of Argos twenty-six centuries ago.

In the middle of the eighteenth century, a road was laid in the vicinity of non-existent Paestum. Three Doric temples were discovered: the basilica, the temple of Poseidon and the temple of Demeter, filled with a crowd of pious oaks.

A meal on the verandah of a modest trattoria. Face to face with the Doric domain, one must dine with moderation. No Homeric portions of meat or craters of wine. A bowl of lettuce with garlic will suffice, accompanied by bread, cheese and a glass of wine. The wine resembles Vesuvian Gragnano, but unfortunately it is a rather poor relative of this noble vine. Instead of an *aoidos*, a Neapolitan tenor on the radio lures his beloved to Sorrento.

So I see *them* for the first time — with my own eyes. In a moment I will put my face to the stones to test their smell, pass my hand along the fluting. One must be free: forget the photographs, diagrams, guides and lectures on the immaculate clarity and loftiness of the Greeks.

The first impression borders on disappointment: the Greek temples are smaller, lower than I expected. They stand on a flat plain under an immense sky, pressed to the ground, an exceptional situation since the majority of sacred buildings were erected on hills and absorbed the lines of the mountain landscape which gave them a certain airiness.

In Paestum, where nature refused to assist, one may study the Dorians in a cool, dispassionate manner. It is the proper approach for this most masculine architectural style, whose austerity summarizes the history of its northern creators. Thickset, solid and athletic as befits an heroic age. The lines of the columns display a clear muscular power. The broad capitals strain under the architraves' weight.

The basilica is Paestum's oldest building, founded in the sixth century B.C. It was first thought to be a public building since its façade contains an uneven number of columns, unusual for Greek temples. Its distinct entasis, the stem's thickened middle section, is the most visible evidence of its archaic age. It is covered with a mighty echinus shaped like a flattened pillow. The upper section of the stem is slender in comparison to the base, which neutralizes the sensation of heaviness and the density of the vertical elements.

The delicate wreath of leaves between the stem and the capital is another rare detail, which art historians claim to be of Mycenaean origin.

The columns, massive as the bodies of Titans, no longer support the roof, only the remains of the architrave and frieze. Wind and storms have severed the top of the basilica. Triglyph fragments reveal the presence of the anonymous builders: a U-shaped hollow made by a rope used to lift the sandstone.

To enter one must mount three gigantic steps. Not everything in Greek art obeys human scale. The temple's inner plan is simple. The central area is an enclosed, rectangular chamber — naos — which is as dark as a ship's hold. Once it accommodated a god with his thunderbolt at rest. It is a place for priests rather than worshippers, the distant echo of a subterranean cave.

The altars at the front of the temple indicate that sacrifices were celebrated outside. The peristyle and pronaos were too narrow for mass processions. For the majority of believers a temple was to be viewed from outside, thus Greek architecture concentrated on the height, the spacing of columns, proportion and ornamental arrangements rather than on new interior designs.

To the south of the basilica stands one of the most beautifully preserved Doric temples. Though originally ascribed to Poseidon, re-examination of its cult objects have reclaimed the temple for the wife of Zeus, Hera of Argos. Once thought to be the oldest sacred edifice in Paestum, it is now seen as the youngest of the preserved Doric temples — a classic example of Doric style — built around 450 B.C., only several years earlier than the Athenian Parthenon.

The temple's mass is compact, yet lighter than in archaic structures. Its proportions are perfectly balanced; the separate elements form a clear, logical whole. The Dorian artist worked in both stone and the empty spaces between the columns, shaping air and light in an Orphic text.

The horizontal lines are perfectly parallel. Optical correction (an invention of the Parthenon's architect, Ictinus of Miletus) was used to bend the straight lines inward, causing a compressed image. The Dorian architects knew that to the viewer the top portion of the vertical columns would seemingly separate and rend the temple asunder. Hence, the external columns incline inwards. The temple of Hera departs from this rule through its facture treatment. The exterior columns are vertical, yet their fluting leads the eye to produce the effect of an inward bend.

Despite these architectural subtleties, Hera of Argos betrays the ponderous and austere compulsion of old Doric buildings though it belongs to the classical era. The relation of the columns' diameter to height is 1:5. The top sections of the capitals, the square abaci, almost touch. They are by no means a decorative element for they support the triangular gable of the temple which is half the column's height.

The temple of Demeter is at the southern extreme of the town's sacred zone. In fact, it was devoted to Athena. This was verified by the recent unearthing of statuettes which bear the archaic Roman inscription 'Minerva'. Constructed at the end of the sixth century B.C., it displays the distinct entasis and flattened echinus featured in the basilica, an example of pure Doric art.

Yet pure architectural orders rarely occur. Two Ionian capitals were unearthed in the temple of Demeter. Some art historians place the two styles in opposition as creations of divergent tribes and mentalities. The Doric columns are said to be masculine, heavy, expressing power while the Ionian supports are feminine, full of Asiatic grace and lightness. In fact there was a mutual influence of styles — contradictions were less emphatic than the classifiers would like. Paestum's three temples represent the three epochs of the Doric order: the basilica is archaic; Demeter covers the transitional period; Hera evinces the mature Doric style. For this alone, Paestum is worth visiting as one of the most important and instructive complexes of ancient architecture.

Noon: the asphodels, cypresses, oleanders are stilled. A steamy silence strewn with crickets. The sacrificial fragrance rises endlessly. I sit inside the temple and watch the journey of shadows. It is not an accidental, melancholic wandering of darkness but a precise movement of lines dissecting the right angle. It suggests that Greek architecture originated in the sun.

Greek architects knew the art of measuring with shadows. The north-south axis was marked by the shortest shadow cast by the sun's zenith. The problem was to trace the perpendicular, the holy east-west direction.

Legend attributes this invention to Pythagoras, emphasizing its importance with a tribute of a hundred slain oxen. The solution was splendidly simple. In a right-angle triangle with a ratio of 3:4:5, the square on the hypotenuse equals the sum of the squares on the other two sides. This theorem, the torment of schoolchildren, had immense practical consequences. If a rope marked with this ratio were stretched between three vertices so that the shorter side of the triangle overlapped the noon shadow, the perpendicular would mark the east-west direction. The Pythagorean triangle was used to delimit the height and the spacing of columns.

It is not without significance that this triangle seemed to fall from the heavens, the receptacle of a cosmic dimension. The architects of the Doric temples were less concerned with beauty than with the chiselling of the world's order into stone. Like Heraclitus and Parmenides they were prophets of the *Logos*.

The beginnings of the Doric order were uncertain. Vitruvius, the architect of Caesar Augustus, provides a legendary genesis which he traces back to Dorus, the son of Hellen and the nymph Orseis who ruled Achaia and the entire Peloponnese. He asserts that the first builders did not know the correct proportions and 'searched for such rules that would make columns beautiful and able to support great weights'. They measured a man's footprint and compared it to his height. Finding that a foot equalled one-sixth of a man's height, they applied this ratio to a column with its capital. In this manner, Doric columns reflect the power and beauty of a masculine body.

The northern invaders, the Dorians, used the experience of their victims, the Mycenaeans and the Cretans. Through our deepening knowledge of archaeology and history, we have come to question 'the Greek miracle'. The basic plan of a Doric temple descends from the megaron, the central chamber of a Mycenaean palace. We witness the transposition of wood building techniques to stone, embodied in the triglyph which was once the carved fore-section of a roof beam. Of course, wooden structures have vanished along with three centuries of experiments.

The great epoch of stone construction which began at the turn of the seventh century B.C. flourished with the structural changes in the economy and society. The Greek *polis* housed rich merchants, local landowners, impoverished masses and slaves who served as the main labour force at the quarries. From the descriptions of working conditions at the gold and silver mines in Egypt and Spain, one may visualize forced labour camps. We should remember, says a British scholar, 'the blood and tears shed over the materials of Greek art'. It has been suggested that these realities prompted the two worlds of Plato's cave, and the parallel of Tartarus and the heavens where souls deprived of their bodies reached a state of blessed peace.

A stone possessed symbolic meaning. It was often used as a venerated object in fortune-telling. There was an intimate bond between stone and man. Promethean legend tells us that stones were the blood relatives of men and that they even retained a human scent. Man and stone represent two cosmic powers, the movement of gravity and grace. A rough stone falls from the sky. Submitted to an architect's toil, to the suffering of number and measure, it soars to the dwelling of the gods.

A beautiful Orphic poem confirms this belief:

The sun gave him a stone
capable of speech and truth
so people called it a creature of the mountains

It was hard strong black and thick

its sides were marked with streaks
which resembled wrinkles

So he washed the wise stone in the living spring
clothed it in pure linen
fed it like a small child
made offerings as to a god

With powerful hymns he kindled life

Then he lit a lamp in his clean house
swayed it in his arms
as a mother embracing a son

You who want to hear a god's voice
do the same
ask him about your future
for he will speak the truth

A stone, excavated by prisoners of war, was dried in the sun, for water — as Heraclitus noted — was the death of the soul. It was then taken to the building-site where the most difficult art of stone-cutting commenced. It was called the secret of architecture, and the Greeks were its peerless masters. Since no liquid mortar was used, the contacting surfaces had to fit perfectly. Even today the temples appear to be chiselled from a single stone. A balanced construction necessitated the knowledge of weights and the resistance of materials. The heaviest stones supplied the foundation while the hardest occupied the building's upper reaches. The period of construction was comparatively short. Temples were erected almost at one stroke. Additions or corrections were rare.

The word 'ruin' does not apply to a Greek temple. Even the most decayed are not assemblages of crippled fragments, a confused heap of stones. Even the half-buried drum of a column or a separated capital maintain the completeness of their art.

The beauty of classical architecture can be expressed in numerical proportion. Greek temples live under the golden sun of geometry. Mathematical precision transports these works like ships over the fluctuations of time and taste. With a slight twist of Kant's view of geometry, one could say that Greek art is apodictic, an imperative of our consciousness.

Symmetry, understood as both an aesthetic rule and as an expression of the order of the universe (hence the symmetrical fates in ancient tragedy), is based on a module reproduced in all units of the construction. 'Symmetry originates in proportion, and the proportion of a building means measuring its elements as well as the whole according to one fixed module,' says Vitruvius, with Roman simplicity. In reality the matter is far from simple.

It is debatable whether the Doric temple's module was its triglyph or half the radius of its column. Some theoreticians see the prime proportion as the ratio of a column's height to the entablature which contains the frieze, cornice and architrave. The difficulty resides in the fact that architects working within the same order express this relation in different proportions. Vitruvius claims that the essence of Ionian style is a 1:6 ratio while Alberti draws a 1:3.9 proportion. Moreover, an analysis of the buildings shows that theory did not coincide with practice. Though one can explain that all values and measures were estimations due to the imperfection of tools and resistance of materials, this does not clarify all the questions.

The search for an absolute canon, a unique numerical key to the structures of a given order, is an insipid academic game detached from reality and history. The orders evolved. This is clearly seen in Paestum when one compares the archaic basilica with the mature Doric style of the temple of Hera. The height of the columns progresses from eight modules in the primitive order to eleven and later thirteen.

The quest for linear as opposed to angular proportions was another important error of the academic researchers, who torment defenceless blueprints with their rulers and triangles. They did not take into account the height of buildings or the point from which they were viewed. Thus the theory of an angular denominator applied to Greek architecture explains numerous misunderstandings and helps us to comprehend the real significance of an art canon. Canons were changeable values which varied according to the temple's size. The ratio of entablature to column corresponded to the height and distance at which the building was to be viewed. Paestum's sacred edifices were situated in its centre and were viewed from a slight distance, which explains the powerful entablature of the temple of Hera.

Greek art is a synthesis of reason and vision, geometry and the rules of sight. This is also manifested in departures from the canon. Where a geometrician would draw a straight line, the Greeks introduce barely perceivable horizontal and vertical curves: the inclination of the temple's base, the stylobate, and the inward bend of the corner columns. This aesthetic retouching gave a building its vitality — a truth utterly neglected by its classicist imitators. The Madeleine in Paris and Soufflot's Panthéon compared to their original inspirations are like birds from an ornithological encyclopedia compared to birds in flight.

One might ask why the Doric order, to our sense the most perfect of architectural orders, yielded to other styles. A Renaissance theorist explains: 'Some ancient architects claimed that constructing temples in the Doric order should be abandoned since the style displayed wrong and unsuitable proportions.' Later there were intense discussions about triglyph spacing, though the problem was ornamental rather than structural. Temples ceased to be the sites of ritual. They became town decorations.

With religion Doric art formed its deepest and strongest union, a bond that surpassed all ancient architectural orders. It was visible in its materials. The marble of the Ionian and Corinthian styles lent chill, stiffness and pageantry: the graceful gods had lost their power. It was significant whether the offering to Athena was in gold and ivory or in rough stone. For the Dorians this goddess was a nomadic princess, a blue-eyed girl with the muscles of an ephebe who could tame wild horses. With the transformations of style, Dionysus, once the patron of dark forces and orgies, is changed into a jovial, bearded drunkard.

A Doric temple should display bright reds, blues and ochre. The most ruthless restorer would wince at such an ordeal. We wish to see the Greeks washed by the rains, drenched white, devoid of passion and cruelty. Yet we must also remember the altars. What is a temple without ritual? The skin torn off a snake, the mere surface of the mystery.

At dawn when the deities of the heavens were worshipped or at sunset, the time of subterranean powers, a procession headed by a priest approached the altar: '. . . Nestor, the aged lord of chariots, began the rite with lustral water and the barley, and with these first ceremonies he prayed to Athene earnestly and threw in the fire the few hairs cut from the victim's head.

When they had prayed and had sprinkled the crushed barley grains, the son of Nestor, Thrasymedes, took his stand forthwith beside the beast and struck her; the axe cut the sinews of the neck and stunned the senses of the heifer, and at this the women called out aloud . . . Then the young men raised the victim's head from earth and held it, and Prince Peisistratus cut the throat; the dark blood gushed out, and the life departed from the bones.'

So it was. Now excursions linger and indifferent guides repeat the temple's dimensions with an accountant's accuracy, providing the number of missing columns as if to excuse the ruin. They point toward the altar, but this forsaken stone stirs no emotions. If the tourists had any imagination, instead of clicking their Kodaks, they would bring an ox and slaughter it in front of the altar.

One must spend at least a whole day in the ruins to understand the life of stones in the sun. They change with the time of day and year. In the morning the Paestum limestone is grey, at noon — honey, with the sunset — scarlet. I touch it and feel the warmth of human flesh. Green lizards rush across like shivers.

The day declines. The sky is bronze. The golden chariot of Helios rolls down to the sea. For Homer 'all paths darken'. '*Biferi rosaria Paesti*,' sang Virgil. In front of Hera's temple the roses decant their fragrance as the columns drink the sunset's living fire. Soon they will stand in the dimmed air like a charred forest.

ARLES

for Mateusz

Thousands of colourful lanterns dress the moonlight crowds in a clownish hue. The open doors and windows are full of music. The squares spin like carrousels. It seems as though I have stepped into the middle of a huge feast on my first night in Arles.

I had rented a room at the top of a hotel which faced the Musée Réattu in a street narrow and deep as a well. I could not sleep. It wasn't the voices, but rather the city's penetrating vibrations.

I walked the boulevards towards the Rhône. 'Oh, river, issuing from the Alps, which rolls along night and day, my desire is where nature leads you, where love leads me,' sang Petrarch. The Rhône is truly powerful, dark and heavy like a buffalo. A bright Provençal night, cool, though conspiring with a hidden heat.

I return to the centre following traces of voices and music. How can I describe a town that is not of stone but of flesh. It has a warm, moist skin and the pulse of a snared animal.

I drink Côte du Rhône at the Café de l'Alcazar. Only the colour reproductions above the bar remind me that this was Van Gogh's *Le café de nuit* and that he himself lived here in 1888, having arrived in Provence to seize a blue deeper than the sky and a yellow more dazzling than the sun. Do they remember him? Is there anyone alive who has seen him in the flesh?

The bartender informs me reluctantly that there is one *pauvre vieillard* who can recall Van Gogh. But he is not here at the moment; he usually comes in the morning and likes American cigarettes.

Thus, I started my sojourn not with the Greeks and Romans, but in the *fin de siècle*.

The following day I was shown the old man at the Café de

l'Alcazar. He dozed over a glass of wine. Propped on a cane, his head rested on his clasped hands.

'I was told that you knew Van Gogh.'

'I did. Who are you? A student, a journalist?'

'Student.'

I see that I have blundered. The old man closes his eyes and loses interest. I reach for the American cigarettes. The bait is swallowed. The man inhales with relish, empties his glass and stares.

'You are interested in Van Gogh?'

'Very much.'

'Why?'

'He was a great painter.'

'So they say. I haven't seen any of his pictures.'

His bony finger taps the empty glass. I fill it obediently.

'Well then. Van Gogh. He is dead.'

'But you knew him.'

'No one knew him. He lived alone, like a dog. People were afraid of him.'

'Why?'

'He ran around the fields with these huge canvases. Boys used to throw stones at him. I didn't. I was too small. Three or four.'

'So you didn't like him?'

'He was very funny. His hair was like a carrot.'

The old man burst out laughing. He laughs long, heartily and with satisfaction.

'He was a very funny man. *Il était drôle*. His hair was like a carrot. I remember it well. You could see it from a distance.' That is more or less the end of the little man's memories about the prophet.

I dined in a small restaurant at the Place de la République. The Provençal kitchen is magnificent even on a limited scale in third-rate places. First comes a tin tray with *hors d'oeuvres*: green and black olives, pickles, endives, and spicy potatoes. Then the delicious fish soup, a cousin of the queen of soups — the bouillabaisse of Marseilles, in simple words, a fish bouillon with garlic and spices. Sirloin fillet baked in pepper. Rice from the Carmargue. Wine and cheese.

More of Van Gogh's reproductions on the wall: *Le Pont-levis, Les oliviers, Le facteur Roulin*. 'A good fellow,' wrote the painter, 'since he refused payment. We ate and drank together, which was more expensive . . . But that was nothing since he posed very well.'

The *patron* did not know the master, but he remembers a family story often told by his mother. One afternoon this crazy painter rushed into their vineyard shouting for them to buy a painting. They barely managed to shove him beyond the gate. 'He wanted only fifty francs,' the *patron* concludes with a deep melancholy.

During his stay in Arles and nearby St Rémy, Van Gogh completed hundreds of paintings and drawings. None remain in the city whose citizens petitioned the authorities to place the madman in an asylum. The document was published in the local newspaper and may be seen in the Arles Museum, to the eternal disgrace of its authors. The grandsons would easily excuse their grandfathers' cruelty, but not the fact that they let a fortune slip through their fingers.

Time to start a more regular sightseeing.

The fertile Rhône valley attracted colonizers from time immemorial. The first to come were the Greeks, who founded Marseilles in the sixth century B.C. From its strategic mercantile site in the Rhône delta, Arles began as a small trading post within the powerful Greek colony. Not surprisingly, few remains have survived.

The real growth of Arles and of the whole of Provence came in Roman times. The town was called Arelate and was conceived with real Roman panache and planning skills. Its rapid development began when Marseilles, allied with Pompey, rebelled against Julius Caesar. The city was stormed in 49 B.C. with the aid of ships built in the yards of Arelate.

New colonists came to Arles: the poor citizens of Latium and Campania, and the veterans of the VI Legion. Hence the official, rather long name of the city: *Colonia Julia Arelatensium Sextanorum.* Perfect roads, large aqueducts and bridges bound the conquered land into one administrative and political organism. After the cruelties of the conquest, the bounty of new civilization descended upon Provence.

The glory of the good Caesar Augustus is still alive on the banks of the Rhône, and people speak of him with as much affection as my Galician grandparents used to speak of Franz Joseph. The Caesar's beautiful head in the Arles collection of stone carvings is full of energy and gentleness. This sculpted portrait presents the young ruler with a beard worn like a black mourning band, commemorating his adopted father, the divine Julius.

The pagan sculpture collection is modest. It holds no masterpieces, not even outstanding works like the Venus of Arles, a copy of Praxiteles' statue found among the ruins of a theatre in the middle of the seventeenth century and offered to Louis XIV. Some heads, sarcophagi, fragments of bas-reliefs, two charming dancers in wind-blown, stony robes. The best sculptures harbour the Hellenic tradition, but many bear the stamp of a somewhat provincial, lumpish Gallo-Roman craft. Here, one has the opportunity — not available in collections of masterpieces — of observing mediocre art, that semi-artistic handicraft, which, though void of genius, is deep-rooted and centuries later, will flower as Romanesque sculpture.

The clock strikes noon. The keeper closes the collection, walks towards me, and in a conspiratorial whisper offers to show me something that is not yet available to the public, but should impress me more than all the sculptures on display. I expect a newly-discovered Venus. We descend the winding stairs to the cellars. The torch lights up a wide, vaulted, stone corridor split by a low portico. It looks like a casemate or an entrance to an underground temple.

In fact it is a Roman food-store: Arles was both a mercantile and a military settlement. The underground storage-room is impressive. To impress me further, the keeper offers information about the disposition of particular products. 'Here, where it is dry, they kept grain. In the middle, where the temperature is stable, casks of wine, cheese ripened down there.' I don't know how accurate this in-formation is, but this simple man's enthusiasm for the Roman economy makes me agree without objection. Now I know what excites the imagination of the descendants of the Gallic tribes. Not triumphal arches or emperors' heads but aqueducts and granaries.

'And don't forget to visit Barbegal,' says the keeper when we part. 'It's within walking distance of the city.'

On a slope — what appear to be the remains of huge steps leading toward a non-existent temple of giants. Yet there is nothing sacred in the ruins, just an intricate watermill on eight levels with water forming an artificial waterfall which moved the paddle wheels. In spite of its ordinary function, the structure is considered one of the most interesting artefacts of Roman stone architecture.

The most monumental Roman remain is the amphitheatre.

It was built on a hill. Two floors of mighty arches with Doric pilasters at the bottom and Corinthian columns at the top. A bare construction of titanic boulders. No trace of 'lightness or charm', as a naïve admirer of the Romans wrote. A place suitable for gladiators and amateurs with strong emotions.

I am shown around by an invalid who lost his leg in the First World War. It is late autumn and tourists are scarce. He has just closed his ticket office and wants to talk to someone.

'The old days were better. I lost my leg on the fields of Champagne, and what's my compensation? A miserable job. Under the Romans I would have had a house of my own, and a vineyard, a piece of land and free tickets to the circus.'

'But in this circus beasts tore people apart.' I try to spoil his pastoral image.

'Maybe somewhere else, but not in Arles. All sorts of professors came here and didn't find a single human bone. Not a bone.'

All right, all right then. Sleep quietly, old veteran, who would lightly trade Foch for Julius Caesar and de Gaulle for Augustus. I did not expect that the Romans, who for me are 'flat like a flower in a book', could still command such vivid human emotions.

The amphitheatre's walls were so thick that during the barbarian raids the construction was turned into a fortress. Inside, streets were laid, with a church and some two hundred houses. This strange hybrid remained till the seventeenth century. Now the houses have vanished without a trace; the immense oval of the arena is covered with yellow sand. On this sand, in dazzling sunlight, I watched a bullfight. Famous Antonio Ordoñez 'worked' with the bull in a cowardly and graceless manner. Thirty thousand spectators, the incorruptible judge of caesars and games, yelled long, avidly, with contempt.

The site of the muses, the nearby ancient theatre is smaller, more private and 'Greek'. The sense of antiquity is not shattered, but reinforced by St Trophîme's bell-tower in the vicinity. The theatre is a mournful ruin, with two protruding Corinthian columns, described by poets as embodying an ineffable purity.

Our forefathers were far less inclined than we to set up museums. They did not change old objects into 'items' enclosed in glass cases. They used them for new constructions, literally re-forging the past into the present. Thus a visit to a city like Arles, where epochs and stones intermingle, is more instructive than the cold didacticism of an orderly collection. Nothing can tell us more about the duration of human artefacts and the dialogue of civilizations than the sudden encounter with a Renaissance house, unacknowledged by guide-books, built on Roman foundations with Romanesque sculpture above its portal.

For centuries the ancient theatre was treated nonchalantly as a quarry of ready-made architectural elements. It was also a battlefield for the old and new creeds; a fanatical deacon brought a crowd of believers to destroy this testimony of ancient beauty.

In Arles, the period of Roman glory lasted only three centuries. In A.D. 308 Constantine the Great arrived with his court. What an ennoblement of the ancient Greek trading-post! A large palace was built for the emperor. Only the baths have survived. They were supplied with water from mountain springs seventy kilometres away.

A century later Emperor Honorius describes Arles as follows: 'This place is so conveniently situated, its trade is so animated, and the travellers who stop here so numerous, that it is easier to exchange the products from all parts of the world here than anywhere else. Whatever the opulent East has to offer, or fragrant Arabia, Assyria or Africa, inviting Spain or fertile Gaul, you can find here in abundance, as if they were local products.' Less than a century later, the Visigoths had conquered Arles and Marseilles.

Yet it was not a sudden descending of night, at least not for Arles which remained a stronghold of the non-existent empire. The Roman walls and columns withstood the pressure of time. There were games in the circus and performances in the theatre till Merovingian times. Untroubled by rubble, the fountain still played in the Forum. The apogee of barbarism came in the seventh and eighth centuries.

The rule of the Roman provincial governors was substituted by that of the bishops and archbishops (a natural rather than a legal succession) called *defensores civitatis* by grateful citizens. One should not be surprised that in these times of turmoil, art was no longer an activity of first importance. Roman temples became the sanctuaries of a new creed. The Mother of Christ moved into Diana's house.

Nevertheless, objects of considerable aesthetic value have survived from the period of invasions. They possess a certain symbolic character: they are the tombs.

They occupy a huge necropolis called Alyscamps (a corruption of *elissi campi* — Elysian Fields) reaching back to ancient times, an immense salon of death. The universal fame of this legendary place — it was claimed that Roland and the twelve peers of Roncevaux were buried there — gave rise to a rather macabre custom. The coffins of those who declared a wish to be buried in Alyscamps were entrusted to the waves of the Rhône. A special undertakers' guild fished them out when they reached Arles, charging the so-called *droit de mortellage* for their services.

From the time of the Renaissance, Alyscamps was a real storehouse of bas-reliefs which were frequently stolen in order to decorate palace and temple portals. Charles IX, the rapacious ruler, ordered a barge to be loaded with such a quantity of these priceless treasures that the barge sank in the Rhône near Pont Saint-Esprit.

What remained forms part of the collection of Christian art displayed in an old church. The simplicity and beauty of the old sculptures contrasts unpleasantly with the bombastic Jesuit baroque interior.

Were it not for the biblical themes and Christian symbols, one could think that they are bas-reliefs from the late Roman era. *The Crossing of the Red Sea* (now in the cathedral) could easily be placed on a triumphal arch praising the heroism of Roman legions. The ancient tradition is vital till the end of the fifth century. It is then replaced by geometric ornaments, stylized leaves. Art begins anew with an alphabet of forms.

Only a small part of the once immense Alyscamps has survived. Twelve funeral shrines have turned into rubble. The remains of the stone sepulchres seem to float along an avenue lined with old poplars toward the church of Saint-Honorat, built in Provençal style with a dome and octagonal spire and ornamental windows in which fire once blazed. The dead drifted toward its glare like sailors toward a lighthouse.

> *Dans Arles où sont les Aliscams*
> *Quand l'ombre est rouge sous les roses*
> *Et clair le temps,*
>
> *Prends garde à la douceur des choses,*

The poet completely misses the mood of the place — where it is impossible to detect any sweetness. This collection of old stones and trees is austere and full of pathos, like a volume of history turned into marble.

It is curious that Provence, a country with both a distinct geographical physiognomy and a distinct civilization, did not create a strong political organism which would have aided its survival as a sovereign state. The rule of the Provençal dukes lasted five centuries (from the tenth to the fifteenth centuries) yet it was constantly interrupted by foreign interventions: by the kings of France, German emperors, and the dukes of Barcelona, Burgundy and Toulouse. This 'eternal preface' (not only to Italy but also to Spain) shared the fate of all lands lying on the crossroads. It was too weak to resist its neighbours. In addition, the hot temperament and anarchistic spirit of the Provençal people discouraged attempts at unification.

Arles was well-equipped in both the material and spiritual domains to become the capital of Provence. The city council was relatively strong and the voice of the local archbishops could be heard far beyond its walls. Numerous ecumenical councils were held here and Arles was called the 'Gallic Rome'. The crusades stimulated trade and intellectual life. When Frederick Barbarossa was crowned in 1178, in St Trophîme's Cathedral in Arles, it seemed that the illustrious epoch of the Augusti and of Constantine would return.

If I say that this cathedral — counted among the great treasures of European architecture — is proof of Arles's glorious past, this might evoke an image of a huge edifice dripping with ornaments. In fact, this church, dressed in a cassock of grey stone, squeezed within a row of houses, is so modest that but for the sculpted portal one could pass without noticing it. It is not a Gothic cathedral that slices the horizon like lightning and dominates its surroundings, but a building whose greatness resides in its proportions — rooted to the ground, squat but not heavy. The Romanesque style, particularly the Provençal Romanesque, is the true daughter of antiquity. It trusts geometry, simple numerical rule, the wisdom of the square, balance and weight. No juggling with stone, only a sober, logical use of the material. One receives aesthetic satisfaction from the fact that all the elements are visible, uncovered to the spectator's eyes so that he can clearly recreate for himself the process of construction — dismantle and assemble in his imagination stone after stone, volume after volume — something that possesses such a convincing and overwhelming unity.

The portal is richly sculpted but the whole composition is controlled by the architect's hand. Bas-reliefs emerge like whirlpools in a big river, but do not lose touch with the main current.

Above the main entrance, an oval aureole encircles a Christ in majesty, with a thick, semi-circular braid of angels above him. A frieze with the Apostles. To the right — a procession of the saved. To the left — the dense, stout crowd of the damned. Between the columns resting on the backs of lions — the saints like uplifted tombstones. The entire composition inspired by Graeco-Roman and early-Christian sculpture.

Among the Old and New Testament scenes, we discover — not without surprise — Hercules. What is this Greek hero doing on the Romanesque portal? Killing the Nemean lion. Yet it is not a misplaced page from mythology.

The Middle Ages knew no rigid division of epochs. Human history was a well-knit texture, a tapestry. The heroes of old returned in images and legends to serve the new creed. Untiring Hercules combats sin embodied in the Nemean lion.

The cathedral's interior is a harbour of peace. The portal was a song of hope and fear; it led into a vestibule of eternal silence. The central nave and the side naves are narrow, which gives an illusion of height, but not of vertical lines flying into infinity. The vault is a full arch, like a rainbow above a landscape. Day penetrates through small windows in the thick wall, but the cathedral is not gloomy. It possesses an inner light, seemingly independent of any exterior source.

Abutting the cathedral there is a monastery with a central courtyard. A small boxwood garden, like a pond, surrounded by a cloister. It was built during the twelfth and fourteenth centuries, thus it is half Romanesque and half Gothic. Yet the Romanesque frame is so strong that at first one does not notice the mixture of styles.

Above the delicately drawn arcades rise the massive walls of the cathedral and the graded roof of the monastery. According to all rules such surroundings should smother the monastery courtyard, deprive it of air, change it into a stone-faced well. And it is incomprehensible how the masters of living stone could transform this limited space into a garden full of delicate lightness and charm.

The sculptures decorating the cloister are of varying artistic value, but at least a few are true masterpieces: especially St Stephen, the first patron of the cathedral; Gamaliel, the finder of his relics; and St Trophîme. The Greek apostle with a beautiful, flat face surrounded by a cascade of hair has an open mouth and huge, wise eyes which sink into one's memory for ever.

Arles was the capital of Provence till the end of the twelfth century. St Trophîme's Cathedral is the last edifice of the epoch of glory. Later, the political centre shifted to Aix; and Marseilles came to dominate economically its old rival. Since that time, Arles has been a quiet country town. A humid wind from the sea blows over it and the Camargue, the soaked Rhône delta where herds of wild horses and bullocks graze. A scorching wave from the Alpilles brings the scent of lavender, heat and almonds.

There are no grand events. The emperor no longer comes. But the calendar is full of holidays, feasts and bullfights. On such occasions Arles is reborn. The Boulevard des Lices seethes with visitors.

On my last day in Arles, I went to pay tribute to Mistral.

The Provençals remember him with the same keen sentiment as the good King René, the Andegavenian Duke, the Count of Provence — the last ruler to defend their independence. He was a typical member of the Mediterranean race. He liked and patronized music, painting and spectacles. He wrote poems and was a gifted jurist; mathematics and geology were also among his passions. Though historians cite his lack of political and military talents, legend does not bother with such trifles. The people of Provence will remember that *le bon roi* René introduced a new kind of grape — the muscat.

Mistral was the son of a peasant; his rule over Provence was truly regal. Moreover, he restored it to life. The poet's father read only two books: the New Testament and *Don Quixote*. One needed the faith of a knight-errant to exhume the great poetry of the troubadours stifled for seven centuries — and to do it in a language ousted from schools and reduced to the level of folk dialect.

The beginnings of the Provençal revival were modest. '*Félibrige*', an association founded by seven young poets in 1854, despite its lofty aims could have been easily transformed into a merry company of glass and gill worshippers, but for the genius and diligence of Frédéric Mistral, the *félibre* with the 'charming glance'.

His first long poem *Mirèio*, published in 1859, was received with enthusiasm not only by his friends but also by the highest literary authorities in Paris. This event decided the poet's career and the fate of the movement. Mistral's entry into literature was unusual. In the age of declining romanticism, there emerges a poet that is the embodiment of romantic ideals: a spontaneous folk singer writing in the tongue of the most perfect medieval lyrics. If he had not existed, he would have been invented, like Ossian.

Its very spontaneity, lightness and natural charm guarantee the lasting value of *Mirèio*. 'I have conceived a love affair between two children of Provençal nature, different in their social status, and then entrusted this tale to the winds and surprises of life . . .'. The poem could be called a folk *Pan Tadeusz*, a rich presentation of works and days, beliefs, habits and legends of the Provençal countryside. The critics' enthusiasm was so great, that for the sake of comparison Homer, Hesiod, Theocritus and Virgil were dragged down from the Pantheon.

The Provençal Virgil did not confine himself to poems and dramas. He edited *The Provençal Calendar*, a journal that outlived its creator; he worked on the systematization of Provençal spelling and compiled a work which today would require a team of specialists. Two thick volumes in quarto (more than two thousand pages) are entitled *Lou Tresor dòu Félibrige ou Dictionnaire provençal-français*. It is by no means an ordinary dictionary, but a real Provençal encyclopedia containing, apart from its impressive grammatical and lexical material, historical notes, descriptions of habits, beliefs and institutions, as well as a collection of riddles and proverbs.

Mistral was not only an outstanding poet, but also a vigorous organizer. His dedication transformed '*Félibrige*' from a company of merry banqueters into an organization which fought for the preservation of language, freedom and national dignity of the Provençal. This cultural manifestation gradually changed into a semi-political movement, though there have been attempts to blur the contours of this confrontation.

In 1904 Mistral, the heir of the troubadours, received the highest literary award, though not from the hands of a beautiful châtelaine, but through the bequest of the inventor of dynamite. With the Nobel Prize he founded an ethnographic museum devoted to Provence, which is still housed in the Hôtel Castellane-Laval, a Renaissance palace in Arles — the favourite city of the author of *Mirèio*. Recalling his early days, he says: 'In those naïve days I did not dream of Paris. If only Arles, which dominated my perspective like Virgil's Mantua, would take my poetry for its own.'

The Place du Forum, despite its name, is small, silent, with a cluster of trees in the middle. Two Corinthian columns and fragments of an architrave are built into the ugly wall of a tenement — evidence of a better past.

Mistral's monument stands in the shadow of plane trees, a very accurate representation of the poet: a broad-brimmed hat (as if sculpted especially for pigeons), beautiful beard, waist-coat buttons, even shoe-laces. The celebrated model participated in the unveiling ceremony by reciting the first stanzas of *Mirèio*, instead of a speech.

In old age fate granted him a peaceful death on the eve of a great massacre. At the end of his life, he was a living monument receiving homage, like Goethe in Weimar, not only from poets and snobs, but even from the President of the Republic.

His death proved his true worth to '*Félibrige*'. The organization began to wither, turn provincial and disintegrate. Though meetings are still held, authors write, and magazines are issued, they are but a distant echo of the enthusiasm and momentum of the first *félibres*. Provence is no longer the exotic country of the Romantics. Publishers in Paris do not wait for a new Mistral. Was he the last of the troubadours?

And no one knows
Through what wild countries
This wandering rose returns.

ORVIETO'S DUOMO

A POET-FRIEND says: 'If you're going to Italy, don't forget to stop at Orvieto.' I check my guide-book. Only two stars. 'What's there?' 'A huge square with grass and a cathedral. Inside, *The Last Judgement*.'

Stepping from the train, you cannot see the town from the small station situated between Rome and Florence. The towns rests far above, hidden by a vertical, volcanic cliff like an unfinished sculpture covered by rough canvas. The *funicolare* deposits its passengers near Porta Rocca. There is still a kilometre's walk to the cathedral, for the town's essence lies deep within its centre waiting to be revealed.

The cathedral stands (if this static verb defines that which splits space and makes your head dizzy) in a wide square while the surrounding houses fade without further notice. The first impression is no different from the last, the dominant sensation being the impossibility of approaching this architecture.

Robbe-Grillet, the master of inventories, would certainly write: 'He stood in front of a cathedral. It was 100 metres long and 40 metres wide; the height of the façade along the middle axis was 55 metres.' Though such description is void of vision, the proportions assure us that we are in Italy, where the soaring Gothic of the Ile-de-France was translated into a very specific style, going under the common name (since the zeal for chronology means that everything occurring at the same time must be given the same label).

In the cathedral's museum, two pieces of parchment (yellowed and damaged, as though slowly consumed by fire) fascinate art historians studying the *Fasadenproblem*. Both drawings portray the same façade of Orvieto Cathedral and constitute a remarkable example of the evolution of tastes. The earlier one bearing the inscription '*manu magistri Laurenti*' ('the hand of Master Laurence', i.e. Maitani — though there remains some doubt about this) still follows the northern style. The stress is placed upon the central section of the elevation above the main portal; vertical lines and sharp-angled triangles prevail. The second drawing introduces a substantial change. Both side elements of the attic are raised, horizontal lines appear, and the composition loses its slenderness while sprawling firmly on the ground. Most importantly, the façade's surface is enlarged to let the colour and ornament, in all its pride and splendour, render the architecture utterly unreal.

Fourteenth-century Italians must have seen the French cathedrals as magnificent but alien works. The severe solids, the upward strain of vertical lines, the ostentatious, uncovered skeletons and the austere ecstasy of stone surely offended the Latin inclination towards the circle, square, and right-angle triangle — that is towards a sensual, weighted equilibrium. Perhaps it was a matter of skill as well as taste. The more chauvinist French art historians view Italian Gothic as a failed offspring. Louis Reau cites Milan Cathedral, a work of many centuries and artists, as the most accurate expression of Italian architectural impotence.

For the Italians, the Gothic structures of the north were creations of a different spirit — to be viewed with a shade of terror like termitaries. The Italian façade was a colourful procession slightly overdone like an opera of sculpted choruses, mosaics, pilasters and pinnacles. Orvieto is one of the most striking models of this pictorial architecture: an ambiguous mixture of enchantment, confusion and sense of total immersion in a forest of colourful stones, weaving planes of brown, gold and blue.

The façade's oldest section has four sequences of bas-reliefs by artists mainly from Pisa and Siena: four great pages occupying one hundred and twenty square metres which are read from left to right and tell the story of the Creation, the genealogy of David, the lives of the Prophets, Christ and the Last Judgement.

The story is both dignified and simple. One discovers that it is possible to render in stone the creation of light (the pointing finger of the Maker, the radiating lines, the upturned heads of the angels). The most beautiful scene is the birth of Eve. A rather portly Father takes a rib from Adam's slumbering body. In the next scene we see Eve, her head inclined, full of purity and sweetness. Further on, the Prophets unwind their scrolls, demons drag trains of the doomed, and the grinding of teeth mixes with the songs of the angels who are perched on the branches of genealogical trees.

A huge, delicate rosette embroidered in marble seems more like an ivory trinket than a piece of monumental architecture. The façade's planes are fragmented by both colour and the precision of detail worthy of a master of miniatures. If Orvieto Cathedral allows comparison, it is to the first letter of an illuminated manuscript or to the high, intoxicating A.

The disgusting habit of closing the churches at noon wastes precious hours in a carefully planned schedule. One is left with the options of a nap in the shade, a pasta debauchery or a stroll. I choose a stroll.

The streets resemble mountain streams. Their current is swift opening on to unexpected perspectives. One floats from the square of the Duomo down a sharp bend to the Quartiere Vecchio. The terrifying stillness of high noon. The shades are drawn; the town is asleep. The slow breathing of stones rises and sinks under the plaster. Two black chairs at the gate echo the coffins leaning against the wall of the carpenter's shop. The streets are deserted. Cats sleep on low walls. When touched, they open their eyes, their narrow pupils marking the tranquil noon like the hands of a stopped watch.

The remains of city walls between Porta Maggiore and Porta Romana. A bird's-eye view of Umbria: Paglia's radiant sands, a blue hill across the river gently rising towards the sky at the edge of the blurred horizon.

Each Italian town has its colour. Assisi is pink (if this banal word can summon the shade of slightly reddish sandstone). Rome is terracotta on green. Orvieto — golden brown. One realized this when standing in front of the Romanesque-Gothic Palazzo del Popolo, a giant cube with a balcony on each floor, whose flat roof bristles with merlons and beautiful windows surrounded by columns and scrolls. The palace has a copper colour but without sheen. The fire is inside — the memory of lava.

No matter how far one strays, one can never lose the feeling that the cathedral is just behind. Its omnipresence ousts all other sensations. It is hard to imagine Orvieto (now an appendix to the cathedral) before the autumn of 1290, when Pope Nicolas IV attended by four cardinals and numerous prelates, '*posuit primum lapidem*' ('laid the first stone'), as the document states, and '*incepta sunt fundamenta sacrae Mariae Novae de Urbeveteri, quae fuerunt profunda terribiliter'* ('the foundations were started for the sacred church of the new Mary, which were terribly deep').

Twenty years after the initial construction, Lorenzo Maitani, a prominent sculptor and architect, was summoned from Siena. He corrected the construction errors, strengthened the walls and greatly influenced the shape and colour of the façade. The great builder remained in Orvieto until his death (though he occasionally travelled to Siena or Perugia to repair the aqueducts).

The question of the Duomo's authorship is as pointless as the question who designs a town (a town, not a factory settlement) which has grown throughout the ages. After the mythical hands of Fra Bevignate and Lorenzo Maitani, the great names of Andrea Pisano, Orcagna, Sanmicheli follow as golden nuggets in the sand. Over the centuries the cathedral was tended by more than thirty architects, one hundred and fifty sculptors, seventy painters and almost one hundred mosaic specialists.

The muses were not silent though the times were by no means peaceful. The town was a hotbed of heresy; and through historical irony and thanks to thick walls, the frequent refuge of popes. The Guelph clan of the Monaldeschi fought against its Ghibelline faction, who were expelled from the town while the sculptors were illustrating Genesis. According to a reliable witness, the author of *The Divine Comedy*, both families suffer in purgatory along with the kin of Romeo and Juliet. There were prolonged contests for power within the town. Orvieto was also besieged by the Viscontis. In a word, it shared the fate of other Italian towns — in Dante's words the fate of *dolore ostello*, 'the inn of suffering'.

The only restaurant with a view of the cathedral is as expensive as the surrounding souvenirs, since the shadow of a masterpiece on your spaghetti doubles the price. The proprietor is thin, talkative with a long, turkey-like neck.

He: *Piace a lei?* (pointing towards the cathedral)
I: *Molto.*
He: (con fuoco) *La facciata questa filia del cielo che della terra.*
I: *Si.*
He: *Qual miracolo di concenzione . . . qual magistro d'arte!*
I: *Ecco!*

Thus we talked about art.

On the menu I find a wine named after the town. The *padrone* praises it more loudly than the cathedral. Drinking 'Orvieto' may be treated as a cognitive act. It comes in a small *fiasco* with a cold haze, brought by a young girl with an Etruscan smile — a smile that resides in the eyes and the corner of the mouth, bypassing the rest of the face.

It is more difficult to describe the wine than the cathedral. It is the colour of straw and has a strong, elusive aroma. The first sip is rather unimpressive. The effect starts after a moment. The well-like chill flows down, freezing the intestines and heart while the head begins to blaze — contrary to the warning of a certain classicist. The sensation is enchanting; and one understands why Lorenzo Maitani stayed in Orvieto, was naturalized and even agreed to race with a lance over the wooded Umbrian hills in defence of his chosen land.

To enter the cathedral is another surprise, so much does the façade differ from the interior — as though the gate of life full of birds and colours led into a cold, austere eternity. The Duomo is a three-nave basilica with the accent on the main nave leading to a massive apse. Powerful columns joined by arches support an architecture in which sparse Gothic ornament is set against Romanesque design, without the combination of entwining arcs so prevalent in the French school. The vault is almost flat, so the façade is a disguise. To the right of the altar there is another chapel, della Madonna di San Brizio, containing frescoes painted by Fra Angelico and Luca Signorelli.

The art of the fresco is ancient and noble by virtue of tradition and technique. The cave paintings of southern France, painted when herds of reindeer wandered across the country, are frescoes. The mode, as though following intrinsic rules, has not substantially changed. Bound to architecture, the fresco shares the fate of walls. It is organic like a house or tree, and through life's natural laws, is consumed by senility.

The decoration of walls must be permeated with a sober craftsmanship. In the preparation of grout, the knowledge of walls is as important as the process of painting. The mortar must set for a long time before it is mixed with washed river sand. At the same time, the sun must warm the portion in which the colours will be mixed: black carbonized wine shoots, soil, vermilion, cadmium. The chemical chain travels from the dampened wall to the air through three layers of grout. The surface is varnished by salt.

The frescoes from the chapel of Madonna di San Brizio were

begun by Fra Angelico, who came with three disciples to Orvieto in 1447. He stayed only three and a half months before being summoned to Rome by Pope Nicolas V. For some years the ambitious city council tried to persuade Pinturicchio or Perugino to complete the work. Finally in 1499, after fifty years of attempts, they reached agreement with Luca Signorelli, a disciple of Piero della Francesca. Aged sixty he came to Orvieto at the height of his fame to sign the contract for the major work of his life. The agreement shows awkward but beautiful concern for the job: '*omnes colores mittendos per ipsum magistrum Lucam, mittere bonos, perfectos et pulchros*' ('the master himself will put all the colours, good, perfect and beautiful') and Luca is obliged '*facere figuras meliores aut pares, similes et conformes aliis figuris existentibus nunc in dicta capella nove*' ('to make the figures better or equal, similar to other figures already existing in the said chapel'). A commission was then appointed to appraise the artistic result.

At the top of the vault, Fra Angelico left a seated Christ and his Apostles. Both compositions are rather stiff and hierarchical as though the painter (or his disciples) abused the compass or lead wire which measured the perspective. Signorelli filled a similar space with an equal number of figures according to his predecessor's design, but his '*coro dei dottori*' forecasts a drama. The draperies hold nerves and muscles not dead fibres. This detail reveals Master Luca's primary passion: the presentation of the human body in action, fully portrayed in the vast planes between the arches of the vault. *The Coming of the Antichrist*, *The Story of the End of the World*, *The Saved and the Damned*, are told in the severe and sombre language of Dante. A certain British art historian, by no means of spinsterly tastes, calls that great master 'virile but somewhat harsh and unsympathetic'.

The favourite disciple of Piero della Francesca was not a great colourist. On the walls of St Francis's church in Arezzo his master inscribed a transparent world permeated with light. Signorelli prefers sharp accents, chiaroscuro and volume to the space of sifted planes. The light comes from the outside. Objects and men are vessels of darkness.

Predicazione del Anticristo ('whose coming is after the working of Satan, with all power and signs and lying wonders') is set in Jerusalem, though the background architecture is Renaissance, as if designed by Bramante. Under distant arcades: black figures with lances, like rats walking on their tails. In the foreground: 'he who will come in secret and by treason obtain the Kingdom'. He has Christ's face, but a demon hides behind his back. He stands amidst a crowd in which the iconologists have isolated Dante, Boccaccio, Petrarch, Raphael, Cesare Borgia, Bentivoglio and Columbus.

To the right, one step forward (as in the proscenium) we see the narrator, Master Luca. His hat is crammed on his head, a loose coat and black stockings on his muscular legs. His face is strong like those of Breughel's peasants. His eyes are fixed upon reality. One can easily believe Vasari who said that Luca followed his son's coffin without shedding a tear. Beside him, Fra Angelico dressed in a cassock gazes inwards. Two glances: one visionary, the other observant. Luca's hands are clasped tightly while Fra Angelico's delicate hand gestures hesitation, fingers *in dubio*. Their shoulders touch in San Brizio Chapel though they are divided by half a century. We are in the times when solidarity was the rule. It was not an accepted practice to question an artistic predecessor.

The Resurrection of the Body occurs on a flat plain. Above, two handsome angels blow their trumpets while their feet firmly rest on air. 'And his feet like unto fine brass, as if they burned in a furnace; and his voice as the sound of many waters'. In the second birth, the exit from mother earth's womb is painful. The scene is coloured by eschatological humour, the laughter of skeletons watching a man assume his body. A surprising detail: Signorelli, who was the master of the nude, seems to have a rather fantastic notion of osteology — the pelvis resembles a wide belt with four holes in the front.

Finimondo is a fresco of immense dramatic power. On the right, the doctors dispute while the sky blazes. 'And the angels took the censer, and filled it with the fire of the altar, and cast it into the earth: and there were voices, and thunder, and lightning and an earthquake.' On the left are gathered men and women with children in their arms. The first victims lie on the ground; their bodies are final, stilled objects. Above, rise the frayed gestures of the fugitives.

Berenson attributes the Renaissance feeling for the nude to the love of touch, movement and the need for expression. Naked bodies, like nothing else, evoke emotion. *The Damned* burns our skin, makes us taste ashes and smell the yellow odour of sulphur.

The scene is crowded and lacks perspective like Matejko's *The Battle of Grunwald*. Naked bodies are squashed together as in a cellar during an air-raid. They are not separate entities but the mass entanglement of opposing actions, the blows of the henchmen countered by the defensive gestures of the victims. Fascinated by movement Signorelli understood its physical and metaphysical consequences. He knew that every action contains the seeds of death and that the world would end in a final explosion — a waste of accumulated energy. Many years before Galileo and Newton, the Quattrocento painter's dry and objective brush defined the laws of gravity.

The sky above the damned is a study of various states of equilibrium. The three angels are like balanced triangles with wings. Two bodies are deformed by free fall. Satan with a hefty woman on his back glides down like a bird struggling in the wind. A true history of science must not neglect the studies of space, movement and matter in fifteenth-century painting.

Finally, one must blaspheme against the authors of handbooks; the Orvieto frescoes are much more impressive than Michelangelo's frescoes in the Sistine Chapel. Michelangelo was influenced by the San Brizio paintings; but his vision is marked with overripe beauty, and his too flexible and unrestrained language entwines objects rather than lends expression.

Great poets seldom find their match in illustrators. Dante found an adequate interpreter in Luca Signorelli. San Brizio Chapel contains eleven small frescoes relating to *The Divine Comedy*, in addition to several portraits of poets (and, significantly, Empedocles emerging from a medallion's black background as if from the depths of Etna). Reliable scholars have discovered that they illustrate fragments of the first eleven cantos of the *Purgatorio*. Not without trouble and doubt. For example, the first illustration portrays Dante kneeling in front of a figure in a flowing robe. The corresponding verse refers to *l'uccel divino*, the divine bird or angel. But the image is without wings, causing the sober-minded iconologist Franz Xaver Kraus to mutter a troubled *zweifelhaft*. By the way, jokes about iconologists are suited to our times (form has expelled meaning).

The bus twists its way towards the station and the town disappears just behind its gate. You can see it again from the train. *Il Duomo* commands like the raised hand of a prophet. For the time being, *The Last Judgement* is imprisoned under the vault of the San Brizio Chapel. It lies unfulfilled. In the honeyed air Orvieto sleeps peacefully, like a lizard.

SIENA

for Konstanty Jeleński — the Alexandrian

FROM my window in the *Tre Donzelle** the view of
Siena is limited to dark courtyards, a cat on a parapet, and a display of
washed linen. I go out early to see if Suarez was right — whether
Siena smells of boxwood in the morning. Unfortunately, it smells of
car excrement. What a pity there are no conservers of smells. What a
pleasure it would be to walk in Siena, the most medieval of Italian
towns, in a cloud of Trecento.

If the gods protect one from organized tours (through insufficient
funds or strong character), one should spend the first hours in a new
city following a simple rule: straight ahead, third left, straight ahead,
third right. One can follow the curve of a sickle. There are many
systems and all of them are good.

Now I am walking down a narrow street; it falls rapidly, then
starts to climb. A leap of stones — a moment of balance — then
another fall. I have been walking for over an hour without coming
across an historical monument.

Siena is a difficult town, justly compared to creations of nature —
a jelly-fish or a star-fish. The pattern of its streets shares nothing
with the 'modern' monotony and tyranny of the right angle.

The Town Hall Square (if we are permitted to use this slighting
term for the seat of government) called the Campo, has an organic
contour resembling the concave of a sea-shell. It is one of the world's

---

* At the 'Three Maids' there is only one, who cleans the rooms, makes the beds, and
in the evenings inspects the torn sheets, embroidering sad songs with her voice, thin as
a needle.

most beautiful squares, surrounded by a semi-circle of palaces and houses whose ancient red bricks appear a faded purple. The Town Hall consists of three perfectly harmonized blocks, with its middle section raised one storey higher than the others. It is austere and would resemble a fortress, were it not for the musical rhythm of the Gothic windows with their two small, white columns. The spire is tall,* its top white as a flower — so the sky appears saturated with blue blood. When the sun is behind the hall, over the Piazza del Mercato, an immense shadow like the hand of a clock sweeps across the Campo. The spire is familiarly called Mangia, after the nickname of the man who commissioned it. From its top one can survey the town with the perspective of a bird or an historian.

In aristocratic times powerful families sought mythological antecedents; later this habit was inherited by democratic towns, who invented their illustrious founders. The rich imagination of the Sienese claimed descent from Senius, son of Remus, who apparently sheltered here to avoid the wrath of his uncle, the founder of Rome. To this legend Siena owes its emblem: a she-wolf. The banner of the town is black and white; these heraldic colours perfectly represent the impetuous temperament and contradictory character of the Sienese.

Because its soil does not contain Etruscan remains, it is assumed that the town was founded as a Roman colony about thirty years before Christ. Governed in the Middle Ages by the Longobards and Franks, the town flourished under the patronage of bishops, and later during the increasing resistance of its citizens to their feudal oppressors, who camped in fortified Tuscan hawks' nests like Monte Amiata, Santa Fiore and Campagniatico. They were ruthless pillagers; it is no wonder that Dante cast Umberto from the Aldobrandeschi family to wail in purgatory's abyss. City councils grew in force so quickly that by the thirteenth century the Sienese *podestà* threatened to chain a mighty representative of the Ardengheschi family in the market-place 'like a butcher's dog' if the nobleman failed to halt his violence.

Nevertheless, it would be incorrect to imagine that the Republic

---

* So and so many metres taller than the Signoria in Florence, boast the guides. Italians are completely crazy about their spires, just as Americans are crazy about cars. For both it is a matter of prestige. San Gimignano — the Tuscan Manhattan — has sixty spires, though the town could be hidden in a giant's fist. Florence has approximately one hundred and five spires.

of Siena was the embodiment of democratic principles. The aristocracy possessed great influence as *milites et mercatores sieneses* were of aristocratic origin. Members of the Tolomei family claimed, with Tuscan megalomania, to be the offspring of Ptolemy. In fact, the most powerful burgher families — Buonsignori, Cacciaconti and Squarcialupi — descended from the German invaders. Liberated from the pressure of helmets, their heads adapted to accountancy; the warriors' bronze soon yielded to the precious metal of bankers. These demilitarized merchants undertook long expeditions throughout Europe, surpassing even the Jews in the silver trade. They became the Pope's bankers, which brought them large revenues and useful church sanctions against recalcitrant debtors. Was Siena siding with the papacy? No. To explain, one must refer to the history of the struggle between the Guelphs and the Ghibellines. From the onset of the twelfth century, these names signified two German political factions: the Guelphs stood by the princes of Saxony and Bavaria, while the Ghibellines supported the Hohenstaufen. Carried over to Italy, the rivalry kept its name but changed its meaning. From a local conflict it grew into a problem of universal significance: the struggle between the papacy and the Emperor.

At the beginning of the twelfth century Siena faced its destiny: a choice between submission or difficult independence. Florence became its adversary (through historical intricacies and geo-political position); both communities hated each other and 'fought with sword and word in refined ferocity, harassed each other in stories, legends and poetry'. The map of Italy tells us that this confrontation was inevitable. The city of the she-wolf stood in the way between Florence (via Francigena) and Rome — the shortest route to the capital. Both cities fought for access to the sea. In Tuscany there was no room for two powers.

An historian justly noted that as Florence officially sided with the Guelphs, Siena had no choice but to side with the Ghibellines. These are scholarly distinctions. In fact the names of medieval parties were as misleading as are the names of contemporary ones. Guelphic Florence often participated in anti-papal leagues; and Sienese bankers could not be serious Ghibellines, being tied to Rome through golden threads of interest. When Charles IV, officially an ally, threatened Siena's independence, he was promptly taught a lesson despite his imperial titles. Both cities had Guelph and Ghibelline followers and these designations often referred to traditional adversaries: like the

Montecchi and the Capuleti, who for generations showered each other's gardens with stones, cut off the ears of their enemy's confidants, and in dark alleys silenced the hearts of their enemy's kinsmen with daggers.

The external policy of Italian states appears more comprehensible and logical than its internal workings. Studied after centuries, it resembles an old clock which stopped ages ago. The Sienese power structure was complex and changed throughout the centuries. The rule of the Twenty-four, established in 1277, gives evidence of the precarious balance of social forces which oscillated between timocracy and democracy.

The Council, that is the *Signoria*, was elected for a short period and functioned as the Cabinet. Its members were equally divided between the *milites* and representatives of the people's party. These divisions did not imply class distinctions. Since the term 'people' was invented, there have always been those who claimed to best represent its ambitions.

The *Consiglio Generale della Campagna*, parliament, was composed of three hundred of the city's most prominent residents, who elected the *Signoria* every two months. They also chose the *podestà* and guarded him like an elderly husband guards his young wife. The *podestà*, the highest officer of state (like the king in a constitutional monarchy, an honour rather than an office), was usually a foreigner. Elected annually, he was prevented from obtaining absolute power by a diet of numerous detailed regulations. Finances, called *Biccherna*, and *Gabella*, the administration of customs, were entrusted to the monks of San Galgano and Servi de Maria — as the best guardians of gold were those vowed to poverty.

On 4 September 1260, Siena lived its finest hour — routing the strong Florentine army of thirty thousand men near its walls at Monteaperti, '*che fece l'Arbia colorato in rosso*'. The river flowed with blood, sang the poet amidst the many contradictory accounts of the battle, as the chaos of combat is systematized *post factum* by generals, politicians and chroniclers to provide rationalizations for dark events. All the bells tolled in Siena. Clouds of ravens and vultures swarmed above the battleground. Processions circled the city; the proud banner of Florence was dragged through the mud tied to the tail of an ass. That night Siena sweetly dreamed of Florence in ruins.

But fortune soon departed with the death of Manfred, the last Hohenstaufen, who had saved Siena with his cruel, blonde riders.

His fall marked the decline of the Ghibellines throughout Italy. Siena's economic defeat was the staggering career of the gold florin.

A radical change in policy occurred in a city so faithful to imperial tenets. The rule of the Twenty-four gave way to the *Noveschi*, the Nine, who were selected from the prosperous merchants of the Guelph party. Thoroughly industrious, unadventurous and pacifist, the government ruled from 1277 for nearly eighty years. Much was purchased during this period: the cathedral was built; Duccio painted his *Maestà*; and Ambrogio Lorenzetti told the story of the sweet life under good leadership in his great fresco.

But the internal feuds continued until the Black Death reconciled the contestants. The terrible plague swept like a flame through Europe, carrying away one-third of the population. It broke out in 1348, casting an ominous shadow on the flourishing civilization. Historians of Sienese art use the date of the pestilence to classify her paintings. 'A gap, a split in history. Everywhere construction works were dropped abruptly in the middle of progress.' Another scholar adds: 'The great epoch of cathedrals and crusades ended in decay and terror.'

'Some of the sufferers died from want of care, others equally who were receiving the greatest attention. . . . No constitution was of itself strong enough to resist or weak enough to escape the attacks; the disease carried off all alike and defied every mode of treatment. Most appalling was the despondency which seized upon anyone who felt himself sickening; for he instantly abandoned his mind to despair and, instead of holding out, absolutely threw away his chance of life. . . . they perished in wild disorder. The dead lay as they had died, one upon another, while others hardly alive wallowed in the streets and crawled about every fountain craving for water. . . . for the violence of the calamity was such that men, not knowing where to turn, grew reckless of all law, human and divine. The customs which hitherto had been observed at funerals were universally violated, and they buried their dead each one as best he could.' This is not a fragment of an Italian chronicle but an excerpt from *The Peloponnesian War*. Thucydides' words paint equally well the terror of the epidemic in Siena, which claimed three-quarters of its inhabitants.

The fall of the Nine deepened the anarchy in this most insane of Italian towns, threatened continually by powerful *condottieri* like the terrifying Sir John Hawkwood, alias Acuto. Violent, frequent changes of government usually give birth to numerous, quarrelsome political parties. Siena was no exception. The victorious faction often expelled supporters of the defeated side. Thousands of political emigrants, the *fuorusciti*, wandered like Dante through Italy.

Emigration conserves political ideas; and one can read with astonishment that Pandolfo Petrucci, the local tyrant who granted Siena its last period of stability, continued to support the *Noveschi* party a hundred years after its expulsion from the city.

Accompanied by a group of emigrants, Pandolfo conquered Siena and became its sovereign, Il Magnifico. Historians differ in their judgement. Machiavelli liked Petrucci because he loved his fatherland and was shrewd enough to use his dagger and poison as one uses medicine — only in cases of necessity. He managed to halt temporarily the carrousel of factions and could swallow failure, witnessed by his short exile at the hands of his mortal enemy, Cesare Borgia.

During the fifteen years of his rule, he constantly manoeuvred between the papacy, Florence and France. Was he a great man? He certainly could not match the Medici. His idea of an hereditary tyranny came to nothing. His sons had feeble minds and were lustful hooligans. He was a Magnifico on the Sienese scale. The clocks of the city strike mercilessly: you will be a provincial town.

Although the sixteenth century started favourably for the city of the she-wolf (Pandolfo Petrucci died in 1512), Siena's agony was unavoidable. This time support for the emperors did not prove healthy for the republic. Charles V, the King of Spain, taking advantage of internal disorder and allegedly in order to reconcile the partisans, seized the city. He installed a governor-general and built a fortress within the walls for the Spanish garrison. With the aid of the French, the Sienese managed to dislodge the Spanish; but the city fell under siege, thus opening the final chapter of its history as an independent republic. Reinforced by the cruel Spaniards, the Florentine army approached the gates of the city spreading terror. The neighbouring villages were burned and trees laden with the hanged. Blaise de Montluc, a Gascon by birth, a Sienese by choice, a rogue and womanizer, barricaded himself in the city.

The siege lasted from the beginning of 1554 until spring 1555. Despite hunger, the defence was heroic and continued even after the defeat of Marshal Struzzi, the commander of the French forces supporting Siena. Women also engaged in the fighting. Although mice and rats were the only available food, the defenders staged a sumptuous carnival. Siena died in style. Finally, on 2 April, the act of surrender was signed. Quite an honourable one, as it included a clause allowing those who did not wish to live under the new rule to leave the city. The exodus commenced: a long file of prominent citizens, wagons crammed with possessions, and finally the defenders themselves, marching to the sound of drums under flying banners. An ecstatic Montluc cried: '*Vous êtes dignes d'une immortelle louange.*' A fitting funeral oration.

None of this can be seen from the top of the spire. But the Town Hall looks exactly as it did when it housed the *Noveschi* meetings; the same black and white cathedral, churches, bell-towers, palaces like huge dark rocks in a tide of houses, a net of narrow streets snaring three hills and contracting round the Campo like wrinkles round an eye. One can also see the gates and walls which do not contain the town, but hang loosely around it like a belt around a fat man who has suddenly lost weight. In its glory, Siena's population was three times its present size.

Beyond the wall the Tuscan landscape:

> . . . Smoke from shepherds' fires stands motionless
> Above the flame, ductile and white; no one knows,
> Whether angels descended among
> Plum-coloured hills to shake down silver olives
> Or whether . . .
>
> Jarosław Iwaszkiewicz

Before I came to Italy, I thought that the old masters were not realistic and that their landscapes were like operatic scenery. In fact they depicted highly realistic, if synthetic, scenes, similar to many Tuscan views and most faithfully rendered.

It is a landscape in motion: an emerald hill climbing sharply upwards and suddenly severed, surprised by a gentle slope which, jumping into one's vision like a hare, becomes a plateau covered with vine; to the right — an olive garden, silver trees twisted as if a storm were raging; to the left — dark, motionless feathers of cypresses.

Mezzogiorno — noon. The sun parches the earth and bemuses the mind. Blinds clatter shut. White flames of heat soar above the stones.

I make a quick calculation and learn that I can afford only a cup of coffee and a piece of bread with ham. Besides, one is not hungry at noon. But in the evening I shall allow myself a gastronomic feast.

A low, sombre hallway leads into a café. Instead of doors, strings of wooden beads rattle pleasantly under my touch. The *padrone* greets me as if we were old school-mates. Wonderful, aromatic capuccino pours brightness into one's head and makes one's limbs recover from tiredness. The *padrone* recounts a story with an intricate plot sprinkled with numbers. I understand little but listen with pleasure, though the tale may concern his financial ruin. However it is difficult to sense a drama beyond these childish sounds: *diciotto*, *cinque*, *cinquanta*, *settanta*.

Time to return to the Palazzo Pubblico. This time to investigate its interior. On the first floor are two vast rooms, the Sala del Mappamondo and the Sala della Pace, or dei Nove. Their walls are covered with the most beautiful frescoes in Siena. Those in the Sala del Mappamondo were painted by Simone Martini. To the left of the entrance hangs the *Maestà*, the first known work of Martini, who surely had a meteoric career in his native town, since he was entrusted with such a responsible task when only thirty. The work is dated July 1315. Seven years later, Martini and his disciples repainted the *Maestà*.

Despite much damage, the fresco is impressive. Though painted only five years after Duccio's *Maestà*, its style is utterly different. The begining of the Trecento is a promontory of epochs and styles. Martini's masterpiece is striking in its free subject-treatment, lyrical softness of gestures. The Virgin Mary is seated on a Gothic throne. Its openwork architecture contrasts with the powerful steel and iron thrones of Duccio and early Giotto (to be found in the Uffizi). Near the Virgin stand two female saints, hands folded on their breasts — a gesture of slightly familiar, yet cordial adoration. The figures of the angels do not resemble painted statues; a gentle line sways them as the wind sways trees. Those who kneel at the Virgin's feet offer her flowers, not cold symbols, and she accepts them like a castellan's daughter accepting the homage of troubadours. A canopy, light as a skein of silk, unwinds above their heads. Damp has blurred the gold and blue, but the tonality of the concerto is pure, like the sound of a harpsichord heard from afar.

On the opposite wall — a magnificent equestrian portrait of the *condottiere* Guidoriccio da Fogliano. It so differs from the *Maestà* that this difference was even noticed by art historians. Painted fourteen years later, it is the negation of the lyrical, celestial *Maestà*.

A man in the vigour of life — stocky, with a common face and clenched fists — rides across a barren, flaxen ground. Over his armour he wears a dark beige coat with brown triangles. A similar caparison covers his powerful steed. Both rider and beast constitute a single body emanating tremendous energy and strength, though they ride at walking pace. Had the chronicles been silent about the cruelties of the *condottieri*, this portrait would furnish sufficient indictment. The landscape is dry like a threshing floor. No trees, no grass — only an abatis of dry sticks and feeble flowers of war emblems. At the side of the fresco — the meagre architecture of two castles crowning twin hills. The one on the left is Montemassi whose castellan rebelled against Siena. There is no doubt that Guidoriccio will smash these towers, shatter these walls.

In the Sala della Pace resides *The Allegory of Good and Bad Government*, the largest medieval fresco devoted to secular matters, painted by Ambrogio Lorenzetti between 1336 and 1339. Abrogio (he had a brother, Piero, also an excellent painter — both died in the Black Death) was, after Duccio and Martini, the third great Trecento Sienese painter. One is supposed to admire this painting, but the lighting is bad and the colours have faded. The *Bad Government* in particular is barely legible. Looking through Enzo Carli's book on Sienese primitive painting, I was shocked: after the immediate, pale aesthetic experience I was overwhelmed by the photographs. A humiliating affair.

Later I read with some satisfaction that the value of *Good and Bad Government* is disputed. Berenson, the ardent supporter of Florence — a Guelph — turns up his nose and says that the theme proved larger than the author, that Lorenzetti could not find an adequate artistic expression and had to use inscriptions, an auxilliary means unbecoming to an artist. Siena's chief restorer, Enzo Carli — a Ghibelline — defends the work, stressing its historical and compositional value. The hero of the fresco is not a man, not even a city, but an entire civilization: the painter's *summa*, an epic endeavour. No wonder the painter fell prey to scholarly insects. In the deluge of historical, philosophical, iconological contributions, the aesthetic value was forgotten.

The fresco is full of important details: slate eaves, an open window bisected by shadow; in the window a cage with a goldfinch, and the head of an inquisitive maid. Clear, well-defined colours ranging from sand ochre through hot carmine to bronzes and the warm black of deep interiors. The massive city landscape, almost phantasmagoric in its brightness, changes into a country landscape, for the first time painted with such breath and tender care for details. Besides, Lorenzetti builds his space in an utterly new way. It is not the golden, abstract space of Duccio, nor the rational perspective of Giotto. Lorenzetti introduces a cartographic perspective. The observer does not stand in one place; he views more remote planes with equal brightness and clarity. His eagle's eye embraces the warm, undulating matter of the earth.

From the staircase I have accidentally strayed into the Sala Monumentale. The name is appropriate since the walls are littered with monumental kitsch à la Henryk Sieniradski, and represent Victor Emmanuel in various poses. Official nineteenth-century painting is universally terrible. Let's get out of here as soon as possible.

The sun casts long shadows. The sunset adds fire to the brick houses. The *passeggiata*, a daily ritual, is taking place in the main street, Via di Città.

To say that it is a walk is to say nothing. Every Italian town has such a street which fills in the evening with a crowd of strollers, pacing back and forth in a limited space. It resembles the silent rehearsal of a gigantic opera. The elders demonstrate their vigour and rehearse their titles: '*Buona sera, dottore*', '*Buona sera, avvocato*'. Girls and boys walk separately, communicating only with their eyes. That is why the eyes become large, black and expressive; they recite love sonnets, dart flames, complain, curse.

I came to Siena from Naples — with my liking for pizza. It is a meal that goes perfectly with wine. Essentially, pizza is a kind of pancake with sliced tomatoes, onions, anchovies, black olives. There are many kinds of pizza — from imaginative *capricciosa* to popular — baked on a huge iron sheet and sold by the portion.

I eat two portions and order a third. The owner of the trattoria is really moved. She says that I am *gentile*. Later she asks about my nationality; and learning that I am Polish, she exclaims *Bravo!* with sincere enthusiasm. She calls her sleepy husband and overweight daughter to witness our historic meeting. The whole family declares that all Poles are '*molto gentili e intelligenti*'. Perhaps I shall be asked to demonstrate a Polish national dance and to sing an aria by Moniuszko. Unexpectedly, the owner inquires if there are divorces in Poland. I lie that there are none, and a wave of praise covers my head.

Above the Piazza del Campo — *luna plena*. The shapes stiffen. A

59

chord is strung between heaven and earth. Such a moment gives the feeling of crystallized eternity. The voices will die. The air will turn into glass. We shall remain here, petrified: I, raising a glass of wine to my lips; the girl in the window arranging her hair; the old man selling postcards under a street-lamp; the square with the Town Hall and Siena. The earth will turn with me, an unimportant item in a wax museum, visited by no one.

2

Only today have I learned who Duccio really was, the mysterious painter whose date of birth is uncertain and of whom little is known other than that he died surrounded by fame and creditors. His magnum opus, the *Maestà*, is just being renovated. I stand in the Museo dell'Opera del Duomo in front of a panel of thirty-six small paintings, constituting the *Maestà in verso*, as though I stood before golden stained glass. The room is small and dark, yet it contains a source of light. The glare of the work is so intense that even in a cellar it would shine like a star.

Though Duccio was barely one generation older than Giotto, their work seems centuries apart. Both probably studied with Cimabue. The three large Madonnas in the Uffizi — those of Cimabue, Duccio and Giotto — are, despite all differences, heavy, ripe fruits of the Byzantine tree. The careers of these alleged colleagues were as dissimilar as their characters. Enterprising Giotto rushes between Rome, Assisi, Padua and Florence. Duccio scarcely leaves his home town. One can easily imagine the former in a country tavern, gulping down red wine and tearing fat pieces of meat with his thick fingers, which only a moment before painted aureoles over the heads of saints. The latter — a feeble, ascetic man in a tattered coat — makes long, lonely excursions, usually north, to a small Sienese hermitage inhabited by parched anchorites.

Only in sexless historical textbooks are both painters treated equally. A critic of definite taste must choose. Berenson correctly calls Duccio the last great painter of antiquity. 'His old men are the last descendants, in unbroken line, of the Alexandrian philosophers; his angels, of Victories and Genii; his devils, of Silenus.' The American scholar quite rightly stresses the gift of dramatic composition in the Sienese artist. *The Betrayal of Judas*: 'Motionless, in the middle of the foreground, we see the figure of Christ. The slim and supple Judas entwines Him in an embrace, while the lightly clad soldiers lay hands on Him . . . Meanwhile on the left, hot-tempered Peter rushes at a soldier with his knife . . . the disciples in a crowded flock scurry away . . .'. Let us add that a crevice above the running Apostles opens like black lightning. Duccio makes even stones move. The image consists of two large masses of definite compositional and dramatic significance. It is impossible to misinterpret the action.

Despite the decorative quality, perfect pictorial matter and the profound thought of this Christian Sophocles, Duccio (in Berenson's eyes) does not deserve the title of genius. No other artist more clearly reveals the obvious nineteenth-century taste of this American-Florentine, and the deficiency of his aesthetic criteria. Berenson demanded from art an affirmation of life and the material world. He wanted to hear a powerful art and overlooked the more subtle modulations. He admired tactile values, expressiveness of forms, movement. He praised the masters in whom he noticed a new conception of the solid; thus he exalted Giotto over Duccio. Today, not without the help (yes, yes) of contemporary painting, we are inclined to correct this judgement.

Berenson was the child of a century which valued progress. 'Byzantine' Duccio had to be out-distanced by 'Renaissance' Giotto. But the prominent scholar overlooked at least two important issues.

Duccio did not belong to the circle of artists who make spectacular discoveries. He was one of those who produce new syntheses. The latter group is often underrated because they are less expressive. To notice them means to be thoroughly acquainted with their epoch and its artistic background. More recent scholars justly noted that the work of the great Sienese brought about the synthesis of two prominent, antithetical cultures: Byzantine neo-Hellenism with its hierarchies and anti-naturalism; and Western European — specifically French — Gothic, with its exaltation, naturalism and inclination towards drama.

Giotto opens the road for the resurrected heritage of the Romans, though their contribution to the world of aesthetics is not conspicuous. Although he worked two centuries before the discovery of America, it is no anachronism to connect his name with the Renaissance. Succeeding European painting loses contact with the immense, petrified cultural territories of Europe and Asia. It becomes a great, but local, adventure, unleashing the monster of naturalism. The connection is broken with the great rivers of humanity: the Nile, Tigris and Euphrates.

Though obviously fascinated by the miniatures of the Paris School, Duccio returns to the roots of culture. Unlike Giotto, he is not a discoverer of new lands but an explorer of sunken islands.

I realized this much later. At the time, I stood dumbfounded in front of the panel resembling golden stained glass, which tells the story of the lives of Christ and Mary. Forty-five scenes remain in Siena, fourteen were snatched by collectors from the Old and New World.

The radiance of the work is overwhelming. At first I attributed it to the golden background which, through bad restoration and a crusted surface, is never rigid like metal — but has its own depths, its shivers and waves, its hot and cold regions lined with greens and cinnabars. To prevent the total disappearance of the colours juxtaposed with the gold, they had to be given supernatural intensity: the leaves are like small sapphires; the hide of the donkey in flight from Egypt is like grey granite; and the snow on the bare, truncated cliffs glitters like mother-of-pearl. The painting of Duccio is close to the art of the mosaic: a plane encrusted with colour which has the hardness of alabaster, of precious stones, of ivory. (Much later the painted matter became flaccid: in the Venetians we have skeins of silk, brocade and muslin; in the Impressionists only colourful steam.) The game of colours is rich and flamboyant. To find an adequate comparison Focillon searches beyond Byzantium and recalls Persian gardens and miniatures.

If the Byzantine painters are critized for their disdain of detail (which for some, equals lack of realism), this objection does not apply to Duccio, whose sense of detail was outstanding. In his *Wedding at Cana* the served fish, both the whole and the half-eaten ones, are very concrete. The master does not hesitate to introduce episodes contrary to accepted iconographic convention: *Christ's Entry into Jerusalem* is watched by a group of urchins perched on a green grandstand of trees. My favourite painting is *The Washing of the Feet*. It is the perfect example of the use of a group. Young theatre directors could learn from Duccio. Some older ones, too. Pictures by the great Sienese could be put on stage. It is amazing how little use is made in acting schools of these studies of gesture; no wonder that we see stage princes moving like peddlars.

In *The Washing of the Feet* Duccio builds his drama like a Greek tragedian. He uses only two actors, but in the background he places a chorus commenting on the events. Half of the Apostles look at Christ with adoration, half with reproach. They seem to disapprove of their master's act of humility. The detail that never fails to enchant me is that of the three black sandals: two lie just beside the wooden bucket and one a bit higher, on the step on which the Apostles are seated. They contrast sharply with the pink background of the floor, and the verb 'lie' does not render the nature of their existence in the painting. They are the most alive element in the scene, their diagonal position and their far-flung latchets give an impression of rat-like flight. The anxiety of the sandals contrasts with the pale deadliness of a white curtain, which hangs above the Disciples' heads like an ominous shroud.

After Duccio, one should look at nothing more, to retain as long as possible the splendour of this masterpiece. It was appreciated by the painter's contemporaries. The introduction of the *Maestà* into the cathedral in 1311 is one of the earliest-described homages of ordinary people to a work of art.

'On the day the picture was carried to the cathedral, shops were closed. The Bishop himself led a solemn procession accompanied by the Lords Nine, all officials of the commune and a great and devout company of priests and friars. And all the most worthy went hand in hand, accompanying the picture with lighted candles; behind them, with great piety, went women and children. And on their way to the cathedral they processed around the Campo in the usual way; and all the bells tolled joyfully in honour of the great painting. This picture was painted by Duccio di Buoninsegna, and was made in the house of the Muciatti outside the gate at Stalloreggi. And the whole day was spent in prayer and almsgiving, and they prayed to God and His Holy Mother who is our advocate to defend us in His infinite mercy from all adversity and all evil and to keep us from the hands of traitors and enemies of Siena.'

One really has no desire to look at anything else after Duccio. Even the *Three Graces* of Praxiteles cannot keep one in the museum. Through the scorched square I sneak to the shaded side of Via del Capitano and follow the shaded side of Via del Stalloreggi. The heat is unbearable. Just a moment ago I soared on the wings of aesthetic ecstasy; and now I want to curse all museums, monuments and the sun.

At last a trattoria that looks modest enough and is called neither 'Excelsior' nor 'Continentale'. There is a nice, cellar-like coolness inside mixed with the smell of wine, onions and hot olive oil. For starters I order spaghetti. This dish is served as an appetizer, as an introduction to the main course. The French start with exciting *hors d'oeuvres*; the Italians act more reasonably, as required by their peasant cuisine which is excellent and nutritious. The philosophy of taste in the Italian peninsula claims that one should satiate hunger as soon as possible and only then think about more subtle culinary experiences. Real Italian spaghetti is exquisite, rather hard, served with spicy sauce, sprinkled with parmesan, painstakingly reeled on a fork, which gives eating a touch of ritual. Later, as usual, a steak fried in pepper with a quarter of tomato and a lettuce leaf. For dessert, a cool, ripe peach; and all this washed down by young, local wines served like water in large glasses, not in those awkward, silly constructions on thin legs.

Determined to escape the high noon in a cool place, I buy *Il Messaggero* with a huge photo of Chessman on the front page. So it finally happened? The photograph eternalizes the historical moment: Chessman finishes his last cigarette. Only the butt smouldering in the corner of the mouth in this ugly, cynical, tormented face.

I must have dozed off since the air has changed from white to amber and the heat begun to ease. I sit on a stone bench near the wall of the Hospital of Santa Maria della Scala, which faces the cathedral. The hospital visitors exchange news about the health of their relatives. Nervous gestures — touching bottles of tea with syrup, sealed with pieces of cloth. The smell of antiseptics from the open hospital gate blows straight into the face of the Duomo.

The cathedral is situated in the most elevated square of the town and appears as a tall black and white emblem of the city, a song that soars and falls in the cascade of sculptures, openwork arches and golden stars. On its left side — a beautiful tower, an angel's spear resting against the air.

One should not surrender to the dictatorship of guide-books but look at this edifice, one of the most beautiful in the world, with a critical eye. After the first raptures, of course. One should not deny oneself the pleasure of enchantment, as the creators of the façade, among them Giovanni Pisano, did everything to keep us in a state of aesthetic fever.

Many art historians claim that the cathedral in Siena is the most outstanding Gothic building in Italy. But the French say, with irony and ill-concealed contempt, that Gothic on the Apennine Peninsula is Romanesque style with added cross-arched vaults. Three portals of the cathedral are topped with full arches; the tympana without sculptures are Romanesque. The battle between the circle and the triangle remains unresolved, and the huge rosette ('O, omega, the violet ray of his eyes') in the thicket of ornamental details sounds like a mightly gong in the midst of pipes, flutes and tiny bells. The influence of Cistercian monks, apostles of the austere Gothic from neighbouring San Galgano (one directed the construction of the cathedral in 1257, eleven years after work commenced), is visible in the plan of the building rather than its ornamentation. Pierre du Colombier is correct when he suggests placing one's hand against one's eyes and splitting the Duomo into two halves, along the line of the cornice above the tympana. Both parts, upper and lower, do not harmonize well — as if someone had placed an intricate, imaginative top over a calm, Romanesque base, trying to force a synthesis of architecture with a reliquary.

One can defend Siena's Duomo in many ways. The most important argument is that the façade was created over centuries and that nineteenth-century restorers did their best to debase the masterpiece.

Yet it does not diminish the astonishment of someone whose taste for Gothic was shaped by the cathedrals of the Ile-de-France.

I close my eyes to recall Chartres. I see the soaring grey sandstone. I open my eyes and see the Duomo of Siena; a cloud of pigeons shimmering in the sun — their uneven, circular, somehow leaden flight.

The interior is equally astonishing. Unlike the cathedral in Orvieto, half a century older, it is not a basilica covered with a roof, but a building on the Cistercian plan. The chancel is cut, the walls of the nave are without a triforium. It is most difficult to get used to a dome in the Italian Gothic. Besides, the one in Siena is not very successful, especially seen from outside. However, it looks differently from within. In its transept the dome rests on six columns. A glance from a side nave reveals an amazing play of intervening planes and perspectives, as if a remote echo of Ravenna.

Aesthetic purists squirm with outrage at the sight of the Duomo's plan. How could one combine the plan of a basilica with a central plan? A mistake, hiss the rhetoricians of architecture.

The interior is unusually expressive, not only because of the black and white stripes of stone. The Romantics were well aware of its dramatic quality. When composing *Parsifal*, Wagner asked the painter Jankowski to send him sketches of the Sienese cathedral. In the composer's imagination this church came closest to the ideal temple of the Holy Grail.

What is the essence of Gothic? Is it a principle of construction or an aesthetic principle of style? How should one understand the domination of horizontal lines and arcades with full arches? And besides, one's sight is rooted to the ground by the cathedral's inlaid floor, the product of an unusual, nearly two-centuries-long effort by numerous artists; three hundred square metres in which one can see the whole development of art, from the linearity of Domenico di Niccolò to the painterly treatment of stone by Domenico Beccafumi.

Moving to the right we pass the black and white birch of columns and enter the Piccolomini Library. It is one of Siena's art treasuries which cannot go unnoticed, even by the aesthetically blind, since two guards at the entrance collect an extra charge. The Libreria contains wonderful illuminated manuscripts and ten frescoes representing the life of Æneas Sylvius Piccolomini, later Pius II. It once held *The Three Graces*, but a priest incensed by their beautiful nakedness banished them to the museum.

Æneas Piccolomini is one of the most likeable persons of the Italian Renaissance. A humanist, poet, diplomat, an author of wanton comedies and Latin dissertations. As was usual for his times, he wrote about everything, from horses to Homer. Portraits of him show the appealing features of a descendant of the Sienese aristocracy: a lover of nature, Virgil and women. He wrote a kind of anti-Castiglione: *The Miseries of Courtiers*. 'Dinners are always served at the wrong time, and one always feels sick afterwards . . . wine is bitter . . . Frugal princes make their courtiers gulp ale . . . A mug, which the servants wash once a year, is passed among the table companions, each more revolting than the next . . . the court holds philosophers and sages in contempt . . .'. To justify this misanthropy let us add that Æneas stayed not in Urbino, but at a northern court in Germany.

After a turbulent and less than exemplary youth, he took holy orders rather late at forty-one. He severely condemned his adventures as well as his libertine novel, *History of Two Lovers*, for which even the most God-abiding biographers tend to excuse him, because of an extremely interesting portrayal of manners. However, having put on his purple robe, Æneas referred to it with distaste, calling the book *Due Dementi*. He was a man of modern times; and like his Roman namesake he inherited a desire for fame. Wishing to correct the error of fate which consigned his birth to the humble town of Corsignano, he changed its name to Pienza. Within four years he erected in this remote place an amazing cathedral, numerous Renaissance palaces and houses — all with the assistance of the outstanding architect Rossellino and ambitious cardinals competing for his favours. There was also a poet who exalted the fantasy of the Pope in ancient measures. After the death of Pius II, life abandoned Pienza. What remained was an expensive engraving. An empty town with a moral lesson.

To commemorate this unusual figure, Cardinal Francesco Piccolomini, the nephew of Pius II, ordered ten frescoes portraying the life of his prominent uncle. The author was Pinturicchio.

An exquisite narrator, 'never pedantic and never profound', painted the walls of the Libreria at the mature age of fifty, at the height of his popularity. With Perugino, he was the Pope's painter-in-residence for many years. A judgement by one of his patrons: 'Perugino is the most outstanding master among Italian painters; and with the exception of Pinturicchio, his disciple, no one else deserves to be mentioned.' Modern historians of art are more severe and place him, rather honourably, among the highly educated, skilful painters of the Quattrocento, rewarded by fortune with disciples of genius. Verrochio was overshadowed by the works of Leonardo; Ghirlandaio was dimmed by the vision of Michelangelo; Raphael seems to be the perfect fulfilment of the aspirations of Perugino and Pinturicchio.

One can multiply criticisms of the fresco (which remains in perfect condition through the neglect of restorers), yet at the same time feel its irresistible charm. Even Berenson, who places Pinturicchio in the exclusive inferno of narrators and decorators, in the company of Duccio, Piero della Francesca and Raphael, cannot resist the fascinating evocation of the outstanding humanist — Æneas Sylvius Piccolomini.

'Bad as they are in every other way, they are almost perfect as architectonic decoration. Pinturicchio had been given an oblong room of no extraordinary dimensions; but what he did not make of it! Under a ceiling daintily enamelled with cunningly set-in panels of painting, grand arches open spaciously on romantic landscapes. You have a feeling of being under shelter, surrounded by all the splendour that wealth and art can contrive, yet in the open air — and that open air not boundless, raw, but measured off, its immensity made manifest by the arches which frame it . . . Now it happens that certain processions, certain ceremonies, rather motley, not over-impressive, are going on in this enchanted out-of-doors. But you are so attuned that either you notice nothing unpleasant at all, or you take it as you would a passing band of music on a spring morning when your own pulses were dancing.'

Pinturicchio is like a composer of whom one can say that inventiveness is definitely not his forte, but he has perfect hearing and a thorough grasp of his instrument. Planes, interwoven perspectives, architecture and landscape create a harmonious, complete unity. In the fresco representing Æneas Piccolomini receiving a poetic wreath from the hands of Frederick III, the foreground is populated by figures standing round the throne. Our glance runs up wide stairs constituting a horizon on which rests an openwork arcade, a fine finale for the composition. Through the arcades, as through binoculars, one can see a distant, finely modelled landscape — feathery trees, spheres of bushes, paths among grasses.

Chłedowski rightly compares Pinturicchio's sequence to *The Courtier*. The scenes look as though taken from 'the book of Count Baldassare Castiglione, written in a wise, scholarly and outspoken style'. They are a perfect study of manners; and, as in a medieval mirror, reflect an ideal image of a pope, prince, knight and burgher. The painter defines his society, its hierarchies, dependencies, relations, not only through clothes or place in the composition. In the meeting of Frederick III with Eleanora of Portugal, we are given a complete spectrum of gestures: from the courtly affectations of sovereigns through the anxious animation of courtiers seated on well-groomed horses; the cockish arrogance of halberdiers to beggars, motionless piles of rags. Life continues in eternal good weather; and if rain falls from dark clouds upon the sea, as in *Piccolomini's Departure for Basle*, it is only a skein of hair blown by the wind over a serene face.

I emerge from the cathedral into the hot, blinding square. Loud guides drive herds of tourists. Sweating farmers from a distant country film every piece of wall which the guide shows them and obediently manifest enthusiasm by touching ancient stones. They are so absorbed with producing copies that they have absolutely no time to see. They will visit Italy at home: colourful moving pictures that have nothing to do with reality. No one has any desire to study things as they are. A tireless mechnical eye multiplies emotions as thin as film.

The square to the left of the cathedral was named after Jacopo della Quercia. In fact, it is the unfinished part of the cathedral vaulted with the sky. The construction of this wing began in 1339. As the lofty cathedral did not seem grand enough, burghers demanded its enlargement so that 'Our Lord Jesus Christ and His Holiest Mother, and the whole heavenly court, might be worshipped and blessed, and also the government of the town always admired'. A beautiful example of mysticism wedded to the ambition of town councillors.

The majestic plan remained unfulfilled, interrupted by the Black Death and errors in construction. The walls, thin as leaves, were erected by a goldsmith, Lando di Pietro, with a lightness typical of his trade so that they began to crack and threatened collapse. Experts from hostile Florence were invited. (Ignominy! The cathedral in Siena was supposed to be a retort to the Duomo in Florence.) One of their reports contained a merciless sentence: the cracking walls should be demolished. But the Sienese refrained from this step, not because they loved ruins. Also, it is hard to believe that for seven centuries they deluded themselves that work could be recommenced. It is just difficult to part with one's dreams.

Through the unfinished nave vaulted with blue, I descend into the busy Via di Città. Sienese streets are narrow, without pavements. A certain chronicler remarked, with some exaggeration, that passing horsemen scraped the walls with their spurs. I was constantly amazed by buses manoeuvring with ease in this chaos, as if the walls parted in front of them.

If anything in Siena is ugly, it can only be the Piazza Matteotti, a huge, shapeless hotel with a stable of cars and a café under a colourful canopy, anonymous and offensively modern in this dignified medieval town. I entered, attracted by a singing voice. The Italian song once again claims its rightful place in the world. It has assimilated modern rhythms but adorned them with old sentiments. Hence the speeding vehicle of contemporary emotion carries *sole*, *arcobaleno*, *luna* and tears. A small, dark-haired boy holds the microphone. A local talent, who in Poland could perform at the Palace of

Culture. Next comes a very pretty girl. When she sings, her breasts heave and her eyelids wink. I drink campari-soda, red, tasting of absinthe, which makes the tongue stiffen and the throat burn. If it were not so expensive, I would have another and ask the singer for 'The Red Poppies of Monte Cassino'. She would certainly know it.

I return to my *Tre Donzelle*, but reaching the gate I turn to look again at the Campo. Everything is where it should be: the walls of the Town Hall wedging sharply into the night, its tower as beautiful as yesterday. One can go to bed. Explosions mushroom above the earth, but maybe we shall manage to make a couple of rotations around the sun — with this cathedral, this palace, this painting.

3

> *Cor magis tibi Sena pandit*
> (inscription on the Camollia Gate)

This day is devoted to the Pinacoteca. It opens at ten in the morning. Thus I have enough time to take a walk in Siena. Only towns in which you can get lost are worth their name. In Siena one can be lost like a needle in a haystack. In Via Galuzza houses touch with their arches, one walks on the bedrock of a canyon; the smell of stones, cats and the Middle Ages.

In the thick shade of Via Banchi di Sopra, Via di Città, among houses the colour of smoked brick, now and again one comes across a palace. This word, usually associated with plaster festoons, small columns and stone bubbles, shares little with Sienese civil architecture. The patrician houses, austere and devoid of ornamentation, give the impression of being fortresses in the midst of a city. Without historical knowledge one can guess the social position of the powerful families: Salimbeni, Piccolomini, Saracini. 'Such a building was not only a masterpiece of art, but a residence and shelter of dependents; and even today in the deluge of indifferent and anonymous crowds, this unconquerable palace stands full of contempt and aristocratic pride, so that nothing is noticed, and nothing really exists around it.' A comment on the oldest palace here, Palazzo Tolomei, built at the beginning of the thirteenth century, whose austere stone rectangle has been emanating undisturbed serenity and power for seven centuries.

The Pinacoteca is in the Palazzo Buonsignori and, though connoisseurs say that the best Sassetta can be found in Washington, it provides a unique survey of Sienese painting.

It all begins in this mysterious period of art prior to the appearance of artists known by name. The scope of knowledge that we receive in school is limited to a small theatre of European history. (For generations we have cultivated a contemptuous attitude towards Byzantium, and with pedantic relish discuss 'flourishing' periods at the expense of epochs of 'darkness' and complexity.) The story of the dead civilizations like those of Crete or Etruria, the birth of Europe after the fall of the Roman Empire, are usually overlooked for the sake of detailed lists of Julius Caesar's conquests. Art textbooks devote more space to the Periclean epoch and the Renaissance than to Sumerian or early Romanesque art. The whole schoolbag of 'lore' proves to be completely useless when we face not isolated epochs, but the continuity of the historical process.

Nothing is more touching than these Sienese primitives from the depths of the Duocento. The remaining pieces are rather polychrome reliefs than paintings. Madonnas with huge eyes, peasant features — solid like the Madonnas from Tatra shrines — or a crucified Christ, whose bright colours time has stripped, leaving only delicate pinks and blues. The Synod of Rome in 692 demanded that Christ's face should express no pain. His budding smile is full of sweetness and melancholy. This special glow of sensuality and mysticism will irradiate the eyes of Sienese saints and townswomen for centuries.

A heated and pointless controversy has been smouldering for centuries among art scholars: which of the two schools, Sienese or Florentine, can be considered older. Vasari grants precedence to Florence, but more recent research discovered a Sienese painting from 1215. A *paliotto* rather than a painting, a painted altar relief portraying Christ, the history of the Cross and St Helena. These small narratives have a distinctive Romanesque quality. It is certain that the Sienese school was well established in Italy at the beginning of the thirteenth century, decades before Duccio. Although the very notion of an 'artistic school' has been called into question by contemporary scholars, it can be used safely in reference to Siena, where we encounter an unusual unity of style and tradition. This fact gave rise to many misunderstandings. The Sienese school was reproached (as if it could be a reproach) for remaining too long under the influence of Byzantium — even though the Greek pattern was broken, Sienese artists maintained the decorative mode and an in-clination toward refined mannerism. The Sienese painters were lyrical poets in their portraits and charming narrators in their group scenes. The city was a republic of poets.

Art criticism is not satisfied with the analysis of individual works but tries to trace their makers, creating 'circles' and hypothetical figures. The first historical artist was Guido da Siena, a figure of strong personality and wide influence, like Cimabue in Florence. The Pinacoteca holds a number of outstanding works by this subtle Byzantine and his school. Especially beautiful is a *paliotto* from the 1280s, entitled *St Peter*.

Byzantine, or Byzantinist, painting is by no means confined to one rigid convention. Only our eyes are trained to react to sharp contrasts, overlooking half-tones. The work of those who succeeded Guido was a substantial step forward, incorporating a greater scale of tones saturated with light. 'One has to capture human emotion permeating the rhythm and the space of these little stories.' Placed against the background of abstract architecture, the story of the Annunciation is told with refined simplicity. The gold of the back-ground is rich, ranging from the delicate glow of dawn to the chill of glittering metal.

Duccio is represented by the *Madonna dei Francescani*, painted at the end of the thirteenth century, that is before the *Maestà*. It is an example of a fortunate symbiosis between Byzantine painting and the Gothic style. The composition of the *Madonna* is casual: her right hand rests gently on her knees. Her throne is a comfortable chair, not a massive and elaborate edifice. The angels are light, as though moulded by the fluent hand of a miniaturist. Three monks, brown and perched like grasshoppers, cling to the Madonna's feet. Wise Duccio, unlike Giotto, did not break the Greek pattern, but bent it towards his own times like a branch.

Simone Martini is absent from the Pinacoteca; this popular and most widely travelled Sienese has bequeathed magnificent frescoes to his home town. The paintings of the Lorenzetti brothers are rather well represented. If the Pinacoteca were on fire, I would try to save two small paintings by Ambrogio: *Town by the Sea* and *Castle on the Shore of a Lake*. These landscapes are unmatched within the Trecento, and few masters of later eras manage to create equally perfect works of pictorial purity. Easier to say than to explain.

Town by the Sea: grey walls, green houses, red roofs and spires —

entirely built of bright forms, tightly circumscribed by a diamond line. The space is three-dimensional; yet 'the refined structure of Ambrogio's perspective does not result from his efforts to rationalize space, but paradoxically from his striving to bring immediately the depths to the surface of the painting'. It is a bird's-eye view of a landscape. The town is empty, as though it has just emerged from the waters of a deluge. It is glowingly immersed in amber-green light. The halucinatory realism of the painted objects in this master-piece escapes analysis.

The rapid swallowing of paintings (in large doses) is as pointless as the swallowing of kilometres. Anyway, the museum guards ring their bells like mad because noon is ripening on the stem of the Town Hall's spire — and that means a plate of pasta, a glass of wine and a refreshing nap. Besides, the Lorenzetti brothers, who probably died of the Black Death, close the heroic period of Sienese painting.

As becomes a medieval city, Siena was the cradle of numerous saints; no other Italian town can claim such a collection of haloed figures. One learned hagiographer provides an astronomical five hundred names. Siena was also the native town of nine popes. Yet, as its black and white seal speaks of contradictory passions, it was a town of squanderers, golden youths and careless women, at whom priests thundered from their pulpits. The loudest thunderer was San Bernadino. Moved by his eloquence, women burned their high-heeled shoes, perfumes and mirrors at huge stakes. Mystical hymns brought heaven closer to earth; but one could also hear godless songs, and Siena had its own poet of earthly pleasures in the person of Folgore da San Gimignano. Processions of beggar monks in worn robes wandered around the town, but just one company of spend-thrifts could waste the stunning sum of two hundred thousand gold florins during a single feasting and hunting spree. '*Gente vana*' — hissed Dante.

Walking down the steep Via Fontebranda we enter the old district of tanners. Not far from the Porta Fontebranda there is a spring of the same name. Because water was in great demand in Siena — unlike Rome, a town of fountains — a washing basin was con-structed and a *loggia* where Sienese women have been gossiping for nine centuries. Caterina Benincasa came here with her water jug. Later she became a saint.

She was the twenty-fifth child of a dyer. Her mother's name was like the opening of an aria: Mona Lapa di Puccio di Piagente. The girl, born in 1347, was a child of strong personality. She entered the Dominican order early, and soon became an outstanding figure in her home town, in Italy and throughout the Christian world, though her legend and her apologists overestimate her historical importance.

Catherine tended the lepers, mortified her body and dealt with politics on a scale one could call international. She attracted a group of lay adorers with whom she strolled around the surrounding fields towards Florence — where the Tuscan landscape is ripe with olives, cypresses and vineyards — or south, to the favourite place of anchorites, a desert parched like a donkey's hide. She must have been a charming woman, though not a beautiful one, as can be seen in her portrait by Andrea Vanni in the church of San Domenico.

Her mysticism had the colour of blood. In her dictated letters (she learnt to write only three years before her death, '*con molti sospiri e abondanza di lagrime*'), two words reappear with striking frequency: *fuoco* and *sangue*. One day she accompanied a convict to the place of execution. Later she kept his severed head in her lap. 'When the corpse was taken away, my soul rested in sweet peace, and I relished the smell of blood.' A contribution to medieval psychology.

The Sienese nun enjoyed an immense authority, but it was only a moral authority. Because she lived in Europe, not in India, and in times of demoralization, cruelty and corruption, her political influence was less important than historians imagine. Her most famous deed was her visit to Avignon, to the court of Gregory XI. In many ways Catherine resembled Joan of Arc. She too was a simple girl who claimed to hear the voice of God. Because she knew only the Tuscan dialect and was unversed in theology, she was an object of ridicule to French cardinals. It is not certain to what degree she influenced Gregory's decision to shift the papal capital back to Rome. More recent research claims that this return was decided in advance of Catherine's visit to Avignon.

Towards the end of her life, she used all her fading powers to support Urban VI, not the best of popes, in his struggle against Clement VII. In political actions her naïve greatness always clashed with her sober shrewdness. She wrote hundreds of letters to prominent figures, sometimes harsh, sometimes sweet in tone. These letters had more or less the same effect as the contemporary protests of the League for the Defence of Human Rights. To free Italy from the cruel *condottiere* Sir John Hawkwood, alias Giovanni Acuto, she asked him to turn his wrath against the Turks. She tried to conquer the world by love. She belongs to legend.

To the east, the church of San Domenico; to the west, another spiritual fortress of Siena, the austere church of San Francisco, with a shocking composition by Pietro Lorenzetti: *The Crucifixion*. In the immediate vicinity of the church stood the pulpit of San Bernardino, whose sermons, transcribed by his listeners, are full of verve, humour and striking observations.

I return to the Pinacoteca.

By the middle of the fourteenth century, the great epoch of Sienese painting was coming to a close. Though the school existed without interruption until the end of the fifteenth century, until the city's final political downfall, such phenomena as Duccio, Martini, Lorenzetti never reappeared. But throughout its history Sienese painting managed to maintain an outstanding unity of style, which we seek in vain in the Florentine school.

Sienese art, though rarely reflecting immediate reality, was closely connected with social life. Siena had no great patrons like the Medici, but interest in art was more popular and democratic than anywhere else. A rich guild of tanners ordered a polyptych from expensive Sassetta; bakers and butchers were customers of Mattea di Giovanni; one of the poorer guilds, that of patchers, had to content itself with what Andrea Niccolò offered to paint. A rare, happy example of the marriage of bureaucracy and art was the habit of asking outstanding artists to illustrate the wooden covers of the *Biccherna's* account books.

The beginning of the Quattrocento sees the emergence of one of the most charming painters in the history of art: Sassetta. His paintings are dispersed throughout the world, but the Pinacoteca holds the most representative ones of this illustrator of the life of St Francis. Sassetta captured the essence of the Franciscan legend with magnificent accuracy because he himself was totally immersed in the miraculous. In the story about St Francis and the poor knight, a tower, uprooted like a tree, soars above the town, the angels and other participants of the drama; and we are not offended by this surrealist effect, since in Sassetta the ordinary is mixed with the impossible. It used to be said that Sasssetta and his colleagues were outdated and did not understand the spirit of the Renaissance. In fact, they entered the new world of the Renaissance without breaking the Gothic tradition, just as a Gothic painter — Duccio — did not break with the Byzantine tradition. Sassetta's art is not mannered, it is the reconsidered tradition of his great predecessors.

He was a prolific painter and often left Siena. He was in touch with old and new sources of art. Contemporary art historians stress his connections with Domenico Veneziano and his influence on the great Piero della Francesca.

He died on 1 April 1450, having contracted pneumonia during his work on a fresco that adorned the Porta Romana till 1944. The story of his posthumous fame is very instructive. At the end of the nineteenth century he was counted among the third-rate painters. Berenson brought him out of oblivion by ascribing to him a number of works considered anonymous. More recently, Alberto Graziani 'deprived' him of some paintings by creating a hypothetical figure: 'Maestro dell'Osservanza' (the name of a cloister near Siena). Graziano acted like an astronomer who calculated the existence of a new star long before its observation. One of the most beautiful paintings of this master is *St Anthony's Meeting with St Paul*. A road leads among forested hills. First, one sees the small figure of the saint with a tiny stick, entering the forest. Later, in the centre of the painting, he talks with a faun; both interlocutors are well-mannered and certainly refrain from theological subjects, as the conversation is held in an obviously friendly atmosphere. Finally, on the very rim of the painting, the two saints embrace warmly in front of a hermit's cave.

Sassetta's brush was inherited by his pupil, Sano di Pietro, who kept the largest atelier in Siena. He could not equal his master (less subtle, and more sentimental), but what a marvellous teller of anecdotes! He is well represented in the Pinacoteca. From Sassetta he inherited his love of red and utilized it *con brio*. The narrative passion was shared by all Sienese painters, but Sano di Pietro was the teller of tellers. One of his paintings tells the story of Pope Calixtus III's vision of the Madonna. The two figures occupy three-quarters of the painting. The artist also painted a muleteer with burdened donkeys. One is disappearing behind the pink gate of Siena. Contrasted with the grave solemnity of the main themes, this detail is overwhelmingly comic, like a *zwischenruf* dropped casually in the middle of a ceremonial speech.

One of the most seductive painters of the Sienese Quattrocento was Neroccio, an artist of delicate colour and Chinese precision; perhaps the last artist whose work still echoed the linear precision of Simone Martini.

And here we enter the declining period of the Sienese school; with Vecchietta and Sodoma — the latter appeared suddenly, seemingly without introduction — we step into the fading Renaissance.

Sodoma's paintings cannot convince us of his greatness, though one knows that he was a disciple of Leonardo, and that his career was often fortunate. Here we see him fat and vulgar; his forms suffer from dropsy. The composition of *The Swoon of St Catherine* is heavy and pretentious; its sand colour is nauseous. *Christ Tied to a Column* has the torso of a gladiator; but the painting is devoid of power and expressiveness, though Enzo Carli claims that despite everything this is the finest interpretation of Leonardo's *sfumato* and *chiaroscuro*. Sodoma was a prolific painter, oscillating between the styles of young Perugino and young Raphael; but one rather agrees with Berenson that 'his oeuvre as a whole is miserably weak'.

I console myself that Sodoma was not a Sienese, since he was born in Lombardy. He was knighted by the Pope and settled in Siena, where he became an official painter. Vasari, a gossip, gives him bad credits as artist and man. He was an eccentric, a bohemian in the *fin de siècle* style. It is rumoured that he had a domesticated talking jack-daw, three parrots and as many vixen wives. He adored horses like a native Sienese, and this passion cost him large sums. In one of his paintings he portrayed himself beside Raphael, an indication that he held an exaggerated opinion of his own talent. His end, in a Sienese hospital, is said to have been miserable. Before his death he wrote a testament in the manner of Villon.

The last of the Sienese painters was Beccafumi. One looks at him with real annoyance. Only a colourful smoke soaring above the once magnificent school. Besides, that was the end of the Sienese Republic. The civilization of the city of the she-wolf was sinking like an island. Beccafumi locks up Sienese art and tosses the key into the abyss of time.

I go out into a town preparing for its daily *passeggiata*, but I cannot stop thinking about the painters dead centuries ago. I suddenly recall a figure from Ambrogio Lorenzetti's fresco in the Palazzo Pubblico. It was an allegory of Peace: a casually seated woman in a white robe, her form defined by a single line, which stays forever under your eyelids. Where did I see similar women? Of course, in the canvases of Henri Matisse. Matisse — the last Sienese?

I talk of paintings but I also think about poetry. The Sienese school was an example of how to develop individual talent without breaking with the past. It achieved what Eliot writes about when he analyses the concept of tradition which we Poles associate, not only in theory but also in practice, with academicism.

'It cannot be inherited, and if you want it you must obtain it by great labour. It involves, in the first place, the historical sense, which we may call nearly indispensable to anyone who would continue to be a poet beyond his twenty-fifth year; and the historical sense involves a perception, not only of the pastness of the past, but of its presence; the historical sense compels a man to write not merely with his own generation in his bones, but with a feeling that the whole of the literature of his own country has a simultaneous existence and composes a simultaneous order.' Also, 'No poet, no artist of any art, has his complete meaning alone, . . . you must set him, for contrast and comparison, among the dead.'

A small trattoria fills with a crowd of regular customers. They enter, take their own serviettes from a shelf under a clock, sit at their own places among their own companions. They eat pasta, drink wine, chat, play cards and throw dice with an expertise and gusto which seems to have been intensifying from generation to generation. Their conversation is animated. Italian is probably the most exclamatory of all languages and those *via*, *veh*, *ahi*, *ih* explode like firecrackers. I guess that the subject is the *palio*. There will be a *palio* one week from now.

The name comes from a piece of painted silk, the annual prize for the horse-race round the Campo. Every year, on 2 June and 16 August, the town changes into a great historic theatre, which would certainly delight Chesterton. Three city districts, the so-called *terzi* — Città, San Martino and Camollia — delegate their own champions. It is a relic of a medieval military organization which divided the city into seventeen *contrade*, miniature military communities; and each one had its commander, its church, its banner and seal. Twice a year emotions soar, high bets are made, complicated plots are woven around the probable winner, and all this is for real, not just for tourists. The feast is colourful, full of tumult, horses and confusion. Yes, history has turned into a costume and war into a cavalcade around the market-place.

I ask the *padrone* of the trattoria for a better wine. He brings last year's chianti from his own vineyard, saying that his family has owned this vineyard for four hundred years and that this is the best chianti in Siena. And now he stares at me from behind the counter to see what I will do with this noble vintage.

One has to swirl the glass gently to see how the wine flows down its walls, if it leaves any traces. Next, one has to raise it to one's eyes and — to use the words of some French gourmand — sink one's eyes into the live rubies and contemplate them like a Chinese sea full of corals and algae. The third movement: bring the rim of the glass to the lower lip and inhale the *mammola* — the bouquet of violets informing your nostrils that the chianti is good. Inhale it to the bottom of your lungs, as if to ingest the fragrance of ripe grapes and earth. Finally — without barbarian haste — sip a little and spread the dark, chamois taste on your palate.

I smile at the *padrone* with approbation. A huge lamp of joyful pride lights above his head. Life is beautiful and people are good.

For the main course I order *bistecca alla Bismarck*. It is leathery. No wonder — so many years.

This is my last evening in Siena. I go to the Campo to throw a few lire into the Fonte Gaia, though to tell the truth, I have little hope of returning. Later, having no one to talk to, I say 'adio' to the Palazzo Pubblico and the Torre del Mangia. '*Auguri, Siena, tanti auguri.*'

Returning to the *Tre Donzelle*, I have a great desire to wake the maid, to tell her that I am leaving tomorrow, and that I felt fine here. If I were not afraid of the word, I would say that I was happy here. But I do not know if she would understand me.

I go to bed with Ungaretti's poems. In one I find a very appropriate farewell:

Again I see your slow mouth
(The sea flows to meet it in the night)
And the mare of your loins
Hurling you in agony
Into my singing arms,
And a sleep retrieving you
To coloured things and new deaths.

And the cruel solitude
That every lover finds within himself,
Now an endless grave,
Divides me from you for ever.

Dear one, distant as in a mirror . . .

A STONE FROM THE CATHEDRAL

THE train pulled up at the Gare du Nord just before midnight. At the exit I was accosted by a little man offering me a hotel. But it seemed sacrilege to spend my first night in Paris in bed. Besides, the middle-man was red-haired, and therefore suspicious. '*Il y a du louche dans cette affaire*,' I thought. I deposited my suitcase in the left-luggage office and ventured into the city equipped with a French-Polish dictionary and *The Guide to Europe* (second edition, revised and expanded by the Academic Touring Club, Lwów 1909).

This invaluable publication from my father's library was my introduction to the mysteries of Paris. It was written when the city's transportation consisted of omnibuses drawn by three white horses, the Polish pension of pani Pióro still prospered on rue de l'Estrapade, and 'The Institution of Virtue and Bread', founded in 1862, still conducted its charitable activities under the presidency of Zamojski. The cultural information in the guide was scarce, but to the point. For instance: theatres are numerous, but tickets expensive, and one should not invite ladies to the gallery. Under 'Museums and Curiosities' the guide reserved first place for *les égouts*, the sewers, especially since free tickets were issued at the Town Hall. The most tantalizing item was a recommendation to visit the morgue near Notre-Dame. 'Bodies of unknown identity are displayed there. Frozen, they can be preserved in good condition for up to three months.'

I walked straight ahead, along the Boulevard Sébastopol dazed by the commotion of people, vehicles and lights. I wanted to reach the Seine at all costs. The instinct of a man from the provinces prompted that it should be quieter beyond the river. I crossed a bridge and found myself on the Ile de la Cité. And indeed, it was dark and peaceful. It started raining. I passed the Conciergerie, a gloomy edifice, like an illustration from Victor Hugo, and reached a square facing the illuminated Cathedral of Notre-Dame. Then it happened. I realized that I would never write my dissertation on Paul Valéry and to the despair of my literary friends I would return home unaware of the most fashionable French poet of the season.

I found quarters near the cathedral, on the Ile Saint-Louis. After a few days, thanks to reduced fares on Sundays, I went to Chartres. Here my fate as a lover of Gothic was sealed. From that moment I used every opportunity to realize my insane plan of visiting all the French cathedrals. Naturally the project remained uncompleted, but I managed to see the most important ones: Senlis, Tours, Noyon, Laon, Lyon, Châlons-sur-Marne, Reims, Rouen, Beauvais, Amiens, Bourges. After these excursions, I returned to Paris as if from mountain expeditions and dug into books at the Bibliothèque Sainte-Geneviève. Naïvely I first searched for a formula which would explain the Gothic in its totality — its construction, symbols and metaphysics. But prudent scholars did not provide an unequivocal answer.

The idea of this sketch came in Chartres when I stood in a stone porch, the so-called *clocher neuf*. The passing clouds gave an illusion of flight. Under my feet was a huge, mossy sandstone block with a small arrow — the mark of a mason. Perhaps instead of writing about stained glass modulating light as Gregorian chant modulates silence, about mysterious chimeras meditating above the abyss of time, one should ruminate on how these stones were hoisted, about bricklayers, stonemasons and architects — their materials, tools, tricks and wages — forfeiting what possessed their souls when they erected this cathedral. A simple goal, an accountant's view of the Gothic, but the Middle Ages also teach modesty.

Over the centuries the Gothic has been humiliated, belittled like no other great style in the history of art. Critics bombarded it with epithets, in the way Napoleon's soldiers bombarded the face of the Sphinx. The wigs of the classicists stood on end at the sight of these insane edifices. 'Everywhere windows, rosettes, spikes; the stones seem to be cut like cardboard; everything hangs in the air.'

The matter did not end in verbal abuse. Napoleon III had scores of Gothic churches dismantled in the very heart of Paris. Barbaric demolition plans started at the beginning of the nineteenth century.

The only concern was to get rid of these 'masterpieces of bad taste' as cheaply as possible. In the eighteenth century one of the most beautiful Gothic churches, St Nicaise, was torn down, as well as the cathedral in Cambrai and many others. There was no mercy for 'the style of the Goths', which 'was governed by a whim devoid of any nobility and poisoning the fine arts' — speaks the encyclopedist, Chevalier de Jaucourt.

Millions, millions of tons of stone. Between the eleventh and fourteenth centuries more stone was excavated than in Egypt. The eighty cathedrals and five hundred churches built in this period, if gathered together, would effect a mountain range erected by human hands. In one of my books I saw a drawing of a façade of a Greek temple imposed on the façade of a Gothic cathedral. It was clear that many an Acropolis could be contained, as in a suitcase, inside cathedrals like Amiens or Reims. However, little results from such comparisons, at least little that would tell us about the functions of sacred buildings in different periods. The temples of antiquity housed the gods; cathedrals house the faithful. The immortals are always less numerous than their believers.

The surface of a great cathedral is about four to five thousand square metres; therefore it could easily contain the inhabitants of an entire town and numerous pilgrims. Since such an undertaking demanded immense expenditure, one should start with the finances.

No written sources suggest that these large-scale works proceeded according to an estimated budget. The romantic mode of measuring one's forces after one's plans dominated medieval book-keeping. Besides, in the beginning there was enough money, thanks to the enthusiasm of the faithful for whom a cathedral was also the focus of local patriotism. Later there were ups and downs.

This explains why so few cathedrals were maintained in a uniform style and built in one sweep. Let us add one more remark. The costs exceeded the means at the disposal of an individual, even if he were the sovereign. In order to secure a regular supply of money, the popes of the thirteenth century demanded that churches contribute a quarter of their income to the construction work. However, this recommendation was not always obeyed. Thus rulers like Johann of Bohemia transferred revenues from the royal silver mines. City councils did not want to be left out. In 1292 an income census was conducted in Orvieto and a graduated tax imposed to finance the construction of the Duomo. The register of donors for Milan

Cathedral has been preserved. It lists all sorts of professions, courtesans included. The donations were often in kind. The Queen of Cyprus, for example, endowed one of the Italian cathedrals with a magnificent cloth of gold. Such charitable frenzy was occasionally the cause of family feuds. A certain Italian citizen demanded the return of his gold buttons, donated by his wife.

At church doors stalls were opened in which donations could be purchased, from precious stones to hens. Charity collectors travelled to distant lands to secure building funds. To erect their abbey in Silvanes the Cistercians sought assistance from the Emperor of Constantinople, the King of Sicily and the Duke of Champagne. Believers established brotherhoods to help finance work in progress. The most picturesque was probably the 'brotherhood of bowlers' from Xanten, as one might translate *'confrérie des joueurs de boule'*. The membership must have been quite respectable as the fraternity included a bishop. One should not overlook the income from the sale of spiritual values. Like indulgences. In 1487 one-third of the expenses of St Victor's Collegiate in Xanten was covered by this merchandise. The right to grant indulgences was not free either. In 1397 the citizens of Milan bought *unam bonam indulgentiam* from the Pope for five hundred florins.

Collections, especially when conducted far from the building-sites, were usually accompanied by expeditions with holy relics, which were great holidays for every town visited. One can see it clearly in miniatures: processions with relics move along streets crowded with kneeling believers. The sick stretch out their hands, mothers with children push through to touch the miracle.

The Church protested against the cult of holy objects even before Boccaccio's ridicule. In 1216 the Lateran Council forbade the veneration of holy relics without special consent. One must admire, nevertheless, the immense initiative, courage and inventiveness of the collectors. In 1112, after fire had seriously damaged the cathedral in Laon, seven canons gathered the surviving relics: a patch from the Virgin Mary's dress, a piece of sponge given to Christ on the Cross, a splinter from the Holy Cross. After several trips to French cities, the pilgrims returned with a sum which seemed to be sufficient for the completion of the work. Alas, the funds rapidly ran out and another expedition was undertaken. Its story could provide the plot for a fascinating historical novel: a sea journey with pirates, thieves and treacherous Flemish clothiers. After seven months, the travellers returned safely with a sum which allowed the cathedral to be completed in less than a year. Not everywhere was the balance of expenditure and income maintained so successfully. In work reports we often find the melancholy statement: 'Nothing is happening on the construction site. No money.'

Another important problem was transportation. Its means had not changed since antiquity: water routes and carts pulled by mules and horses. If the quarry was not far from the construction site, like Chartres, one team delivered daily a small portion of stone, fifteen hundred kilograms, roughly one cubic metre.

A French proverb says: 'a half-destroyed castle is a half-built castle'. More than one stone for a Gothic cathedral came from the fortifications and civilian buildings of the Roman Empire. In order to erect the huge church of St Alban, the remains of the ancient town of Verulanium were demolished. The examples can be multiplied. Chronicles record instances of miraculous discoveries of deposits of building materials, as in Pontoise, which aided the construction of Saint-Denis. But it was not a common occurrence. Ancient columns, capitals, blocks of pink and white marble were shipped down the Rhine, the Rhône and the Arno. Proud and mighty Venice sent its sailing-ships in search of building materials for the construction of San Marco as far as Sicily, Athens, Constantinople, Asia Minor, even Africa.

What were the transportation costs? If the material came from places a hundred kilometres away, its price rose four or five times. In the Caen quarry a unit of stone cost one pound, six shillings and eight pence. When it arrived at Norwich, its price was four pounds, eight shillings and eight pence. The demolition of old buildings was not blind vandalism but a hard economic necessity. It was understood quite early that the only way of reducing transportation costs was to refine the material at the quarries so that it could be delivered directly to the building-site ready for use, lighter than the irregular, rough blocks. Stonemasons and craftsmen went to quarries where they laboured under the guidance of architects. This increasingly popular practice led in Britain to the birth of businesses producing ready-made blocks or even sculptures.

One should not ignore the most original means of transportation, which probably existed only in the Middle Ages: the backs and shoulders of faithful volunteers. Before pilgrims reached the famous San Diago di Compostella, everybody was given a portion of

limestone in the town of Triacastella, which they had to transport to
the kilns in Castaneda. A frequently-quoted letter to Abbot Haimon
of Chartres, dating from 1145, describes a crowd of men and women
of all estates (which more critical commentators take as a metaphor)
pulling carts full of 'wine, wheat, stone, wood and other things
necessary for life and building of the church'. Thousands marched in
great silence. On reaching their destination they sung hymns and
confessed their sins. This picture of voluntary work is complemented by many other literary texts. During the construction of
the cathedral in Vézelay, Bertha, the wife of Duke Girat de Rous-
sillon leaves her marital bed at night. Full of suspicion, the Duke
follows his spouse:

> *Et voit venir de loign la dame et ses ancelles*
> *Et de ses plus privées pucelles damoiselles,*
> *Qui venoient tout chargié de sablon et d'arène*
> *Si qu'elles ne pouvoient monter fort qu'à grant peine.*

However, one should be ruthless with these charming stories,
even though they were undoubtedly truthful in rendering the mood,
social background, and the miraculous atmosphere surrounding the
construction of cathedrals. But do they have any bearing on the
progress of the construction itself? Careful scholars voice doubts.
The masses inspired by the purest enthusiasm were certainly not the
decisive factor in the great architectural battle. Not chronicles, but
stained glass, miniatures and prints are the best source of information
about the fate of the material when it finally reached the construction
site. The theme of the Tower of Babel, much favoured in the Middle
Ages, provides particularly valuable suggestions.

Stones and mortar were carried by workers on their shoulders, or
hoisted by a simple system of pulleys. Huge ramps resting on the
ground and used since antiquity could not be constructed due to the
density of buildings surrounding the cathedrals. Scaffolding did not
rest on the ground. It resembled swallows' nests hanging at dazzling
heights. At the top of unfinished walls one could see cranes and
primitive lifts. Ropes carrying stones were reeled on drums below,
like those of village wells today. Great wheels, moved by workers'
feet were also used. Churches in Alsace and English cathedrals hold
collections of these simple machines. Nothing indicates that the
Middle Ages witnessed the invention of anything which could
replace or even alleviate the effort of human muscles. Gothic

cathedrals were the work of man's hands in the most literal sense.

The range of tools was also very basic: a saw to cut sandstone blocks, different hammers with sharp or blunt heads, trowels, and measuring tools — set square, angle-gauge, plumb-line. It is not certain when the broad-edged chisel appeared. Probably as late as the fourteenth century. The cathedral builders' tool-kit was not much different from that of the builders of the Acropolis.

That was not, however, the primary factor slowing down the work. The weak points of these ambitious endeavours were finances and transportation (*lenta convectico columnarum*). The construction of the cathedral at Chartres lasted fifty years, at Amiens — sixty, Notre-Dame — eighty, Reims — ninety, Bourges — one hundred years. Almost no cathedral was finished in the lifetime of those who dreamt of their spires in the clouds.

The outstanding Belgian medievalist, Henri Pirenne, drew an analogy between the dynamism of European society in the eleventh and twelfth centuries and of mid-nineteenth century America. The construction of the great Gothic cathedrals is unthinkable without the development of cities and changes in the economic structure. Land ceases to be the sole source of wealth; the value of commodities grows, trade develops, banks are founded.

The Church looked unfavourably upon those who established fortunes not through physical labour or inheritance, but through intelligent schemes. Such people in turn had little choice but to offer a part of their income for some sublime purpose. Though it is perhaps a partial truth, one can risk saying that Gothic buildings were born of the ill-conscience of the young bourgeoisie.

The cathedrals were objects of pride and tokens of power visible from a distance. And also places for meetings and activities of quite secular character. Medieval man felt at home in a church. He ate, slept and talked there without raising his voice; and because there were no benches, people could walk around freely and were ready to find shelter from inclement weather. Church interdictions on secular meetings in churches indicate that they were fairly frequent. The fact that town halls were not built in many towns with cathedrals or large churches seems to support this thesis. Stained glass windows exalted not only the lives of saints but, if we may compare great with small, functioned as advertising signs for mercers, carpenters and cobblers. We know that a good location for a donated stained glass window was the object of a bitter struggle. 'Good' meant closest to the eyes of a potential customer.

It is remarkable that kings and dukes played so modest a role in the construction of cathedrals, especially as regards personal involvement in work in progress. With the exception of exclusively royal temples, like Sainte-Chapelle or Westminster, a monarch's role was usually limited to financial donations, rare visits to building-sites, and occasionally sending court architects to give advice. That was all.

In England, France and Germany the fate of these projects remained the concern of abbots and bishops; in Italy, city councils. Abbot Suger symbolized those who sacrificed their time, energy and talent for a cathedral. One can easily envision him in discussions with goldsmiths and painters, deciding about the iconography of stained glass, climbing scaffolding, leading expeditions of lumberjacks to the forest in search of suitable timber. Thanks to him the construction of Saint-Denis took only three years and three weeks, a record unchallenged for many centuries. Sully was another such patron for Notre-Dame, Bishop Evrart de Fouilloy for Amiens, Gautier de Mortagne for Auxerre.

But one man's unlimited energy and enthusiasm could not secure adequate supervision for such immense endeavours. Institutions were founded, differently named in different countries: *fabrique*, *oeuvre*, *werk*, work, *opera*. They looked after the management and accounts, controlled funds, hired artists and workers, kept plans. Chapters delegated one or two clergymen who were then called *custos fabricae*, *magister fabricae*, *magister operis*. They were not technicians, as one might guess from those names, but administrators. The administration in turn divided and specialized. In France *la fabrique* controlled the financial, *l'oeuvre* the technical side of construction. In time these new organisms gained considerable autonomy, especially in Italy where city councils played a decisive role in the construction of cathedrals.

Let us look more closely at the people working on a building-site. They constituted a small, hierarchial society. At the bottom of this pyramid we see workers, depicted in miniatures climbing ladders, carrying stones and mortar in yokes or patiently turning the wheels of pulleys. They were mainly runaway peasants, sons from large families, who set off for towns in search of bread and freedom. The unskilled did the hardest work: digging foundations sometimes as deep as ten metres, and transporting materials. They were spurred by the hope, especially the younger and more enterprising ones, that one day someone else would take over their toil and that they would lay stones at the top of the cathedral. Economic incentives played an important role. A stone-porter or a digger earned seven denari a day; a stone-layer, twenty-two denari.

Should we be surprised that they looked with animosity at those who volunteered for this work, like His Grace Renaud de Montauban who sought expiation for his sins in hard labour? *Chanson de geste des quatre fils Aymon* says that when the workers collected their daily pay in the evening, Renaud took only one denarius. Not that he was a light worker. On the contrary, he worked like three men, so that the stonemasons vied for his help. He was called 'the worker of St Peter', but after eight days despairing companions hit him over the head with a heavy mallet and threw his body into the Rhine. The important lesson of this bloody story: the number of unskilled labourers was large and the struggle for employment was ruthless. The proportion of unskilled to skilled was probably greater than four to one. The abbots of Ramsey sneered at those who sought employment not out of piety, but for love of money, *'par l'amour de la paie'*, but we don't find it shocking.

Viewed from the outside, we might think that an abyss divided foremen from workers; yet this was not so. Gothic cathedrals were great improvisations, demanding almost an organic bond between the participants. Such a bond resulted from the very nature of the material. A stone, hewn on the ground, had to reach a precise spot above; unlike a brick, it was not an interchangeable element. That is probably why accounts — organized not according to pay differentials, but modelled on farm-estates book-keeping — show evidence of clearly defined work units. Immediately below the foreman was the stone-layer. We see his assistants — *valets, compagnons, serviteurs* — who had to learn the trade, even if unwillingly, and perform such simple tasks as mixing mortar. Plaster craftsmen can be found in a list of trades compiled by Etienne Boileau.

The group above the assistants included bricklayers and artisans working in stone, wood, lead or iron. They were the constructors. Stone-setters had the responsible job of fitting the stones. Their names are well represented in the English terms: 'setter' and 'layer'. Their skills determined whether an arch would resist the weight of a vault, whether a keystone would not crack. Miniatures portray them at the top of cathedrals with trowels, levels, plumb-lines. Their names disappear from the paylists in winter, when they abandoned the building-site, leaving the walls protected with straw and twigs to keep the cold and damp away.

We know next to nothing about those who worked in quarries. They are rarely mentioned and their trade is absent from Etienne Boileau's detailed register. They were underpaid and worked under the worst conditions — the unknown soldiers of the cathedral-building crusades. Yet without them, working in the dark and damp, without them, who cut the moulds of the cathedrals in rock, what was created to enchant human eyes would be unthinkable.

The quarries were usually exploited before the digging of foundations. Eight workers toiled under the direction of a foreman who was paid much better than they, and per piece of cut stone. Their speed of work must have been considerable, as we can deduce from reports from the quarries of the Cistercian abbey in King's Vale in Cheshire. During these years, thirty-five tons of stone were excavated; a loaded cart left the quarry every fifteen minutes.

In 1277 Walter de Chereford, the head of works in King's Vale, had the idea of building a barn for stonemasons. He did not expect that the future 'French loge' would have a brilliant political career. Its beginnings were prosaic and practical. Its purpose was to provide for those who cut stone and prepared fragments of sculptures a place to take their meals and shelter from the elements. The first consisted of fourteen hundred planks, so it was rather small, with primitive arrangements. One did not just live in a lodge, it was also the place of professional discussion. A document exists concerning the intervention of the bishop's guard, summoned to temper the emotions of the disputing craftsmen. This took place not in England but in France during the construction of Notre-Dame, as the habit of building lodges quickly spread to other countries.

In Van Eyck's painting of St Barbara, the patron saint of builders, the lodge, or simply a barn, looks like a bird-cage beside the huge temple. In fact, it could hold no more than twenty tradesmen. And they were truly like transient birds. The times knew no passports, so they often crossed the English Channel, the Rhine, and even ventured to Palestine with the crusaders. Sometimes they were taken along by an architect like Etienne de Bonneuille when he went to build the cathedral in Uppsala. The peregrinations of workers were caused not only by the need for adventure, but also by the search for better working conditions. Sometimes they fled from forced labour.

On royal orders, English sheriffs conscripted masons and construction workers who were needed for the erection of castles, often hundreds of miles from their homes. And for an indefinite period. Cathedral builders, on the other hand, were free people.

Those who worked in stone were covered by a single French term *tailleurs de pierre*, referring to those who cut stone as well as those who made rosettes, arches, even sculpted statues. One of the mysteries of Gothic architecture is the fact, unimaginable to us, that these sculptors were not considered artists. They merged with the anonymous mass of stonemasons. Their personalities were bridled by the architect and the theologian. The Council of Nice decided in 787 that art was the matter of the artist, but the composition — or content, as we would say today — belonged to the Fathers. The sentence must have had more than declarative value since in 1306 a sculptor named Tideman was forced to remove from a London church his figure of Christ, which was found to be contrary to tradition, and even to return his fee.

The terminology used to denote craftsmen is rather inadequate and misleading. Often it is not based on the function, but on the materials. Thus the English term 'hard hewers' refers to artisans who worked in heavy stone from vicinities such as Kent, as opposed to those who chiselled delicate stone suitable for sculptures, called 'free-stone masons'. (Later the shortened form 'freemasons' was used and its French derivation, *franc-maçon*, though the latter was unknown in the Middle Ages and came into use only in the times of speculative freemasonry in the eighteenth century.) When we stand in front of the royal portal in Chartres, it is easy to see that the figures are made of a different stone, with a much finer grain, than the walls.

Work was regulated by the sundial. It started in the morning and stopped at dusk. English builders, as we can read in documents of the second half of the sixteenth century, had one hour for lunch, with a fifteen minute break in the afternoon in winter. In summer: one hour for lunch and two thirty-minute breaks. In winter they worked eight to ten hours, in summer twelve hours. There were fifty holidays which, together with Sundays, gave about two hundred and fifty days of effective labour.

In order to attract skilled workers lodging was offered in the inns. The first hotel for workers, *hospicium lathomorum*, with its own kitchen, appeared near Eton late in the seventeenth century.

The payroll was diverse. Knoop and Jones listed no less than seventeen different fees for builders in Caernarvon in the years 1278–80. Unskilled workers were paid each evening. The craftsmen received their wages on Saturdays.

How much did they earn? A difficult question. We know how easy it is to prepare misleading tables, which will clearly demonstrate that we are fine, or have been better, or that it is much better elsewhere. The matter is even more complicated when we consider a remote epoch. The minimum for human existence is relative. Citing the work of a seemingly impartial French scholar, Pierre du Colombier, we shall only say that the material situation of workers in the Middle Ages was far better than at the end of the nineteenth century. One must add that this is true only for skilled labourers, not those who drilled tunnels in the quarries. After meticulous research, Baissel proved that in order to buy three hundred and sixty kilograms of wheat, a worker had to work twelve days in the fourteenth century, twenty days in 1500, and twenty-two in 1882.

There is an even more convincing indicator: a comparison of the salary of a London builder who ate his meals at work, with that of a worker who dined at his own expense. The former received a third less than the latter. In the sixteenth century, one half less. Contemporary research on the working man's family budget demonstrates that considerably more than a third is spent on food.

Only a few records allow us to probe the relation between employer and employee. In the twelfth century a strike took place during the construction of an abbey in Obazin. The workers, unable to stand a prolonged fast, bought a hog and ate a portion, hiding the rest. Abbot Stedan discovered the meat and ordered that it be thrown away. Next day the workers refused to work, and even insulted the Abbot. In return he warned them that he would find other labourers, better equipped to check their bodily desires and build God's house. It ended with the rebellious staff humbling themselves in front of the Abbot. In Siena there was a thirty-year lawsuit over wine from the vineyards belonging to the construction board, which the builders wanted to receive during their work. They substantiated their claim quite logically, saying that they did not want to interrupt their work in order to wet their lips. In the end the board acquiesced to these legitimate human demands.

According to medieval tradition, the cathedral builders descend from the builders of King Solomon's temple. An ancestry as noble as it is mystical. In contemporary novels about medieval architects, they are surrounded with an aura of mystery; half magicians, half alchemists, astronomers of cross-vaults, mysterious men, who came from far away carrying esoteric knowledge of perfect proportions and well-guarded secrets of construction. In reality the beginnings of this profession were extremely modest. An architect was lost amidst a crowd of anonymous craftsmen. In medieval texts the very term 'architect' is somewhat vague and equivocal, reflecting his ambiguous position and role. Most frequently he was a builder and mason, who did manual work just like the others. On occasion the role of architect was assumed by the patron himself, a bishop or an abbot, a learned man who had travelled widely. Cathedrals were often replicas of existing temples.

The role of an architect became more defined and his importance grew along with the Gothic cathedrals. His position was well-established by the middle of the thirteenth century. But just at this time we come across a text which makes our eyebrows rise. Nicolas de Biard, a moralist and preacher, speaks with indignation: 'It has become a habit that one of the masters directs the works by word only, but scarcely ever lends a hand; despite this his pay is higher than that of the others.' And further on, he exclaims with contempt that an architect, wearing gloves and equipped with a rod, commands: 'You should cut stone in such and such a manner', yet he himself does not work. 'Just like some prelates of today,' adds Nicolas de Biard to make his condemnation complete.

The above text proves that the emancipation of the new profession was by no means easy. Architecture was not a university subject. Among the experienced masters there were amateurs who joined the trade, like the famous Perrault, who 'from a bad doctor became a good architect', or Wren, a mathematician and astronomer, or the playwright Vanbrugh. But they were at least, as we would say today, intellectuals. According to Peach there were also simple men, like the illiterate village bricklayer who erected a large church with a dome on Malta. Monasteries, too, specialized in the trade. In the Middle Ages the Cistercians had a reputation as builders, which gave occasion to a quarrel between the Pope and Frederick II, who forced the Cistercians to build his castles.

Architecture was denied a place among the liberal arts. No doubt it hurt the architects, who tried to compensate for the injustice through the arrogation of academic degrees, such as *magister cementariorum* or *magister lapidorum*. We know that the practice evoked protests from the Paris *palestra*, who refused to lower themselves to the level of bricklayers. (Poor lawyers, what has remained of their causistry but the theme of comedies.)

But the supreme accolade was the inscription on the tomb of Pierre de Montreuil, architect of Saint-Louis, the creator of Sainte-Chapelle. He is called not only the flower of good conduct, but also *docteur ès pierres* — a title never used before or after. This is, however, the apogee of an individual career, which should not overshadow its modest beginnings.

What is an architect for us? One who makes plans. Were the plans of medieval cathedrals preserved? Only from the middle of the thirteenth century. The invaluable album of Villard de Honnecourt dates from this time. I shall talk about it in a moment. Although a plan of the Abbey of Saint-Gall is preserved from the eleventh century and a plan of the water system for the Abbey of Canterbury from the twelfth century, they can hardly be called plans due to their naïve perspective, resembling children's drawings. The lack of primary sources for historians of architecture can easily be explained by the high cost of parchment. Perhaps plans were made on other, less durable materials? Or perhaps — the second blasphemy against the cathedral builders, after the lack of an estimated budget mentioned above — the outline of the construction was born rather vaguely in mind.

The firms dealing with the construction of cathedrals in Strasbourg, Cologne, Orvieto, Vienna, Florence and Siena enviously guarded the blueprints which appeared in large numbers in the fourteenth and fifteenth centuries. This is the time of 'tracing houses', *chambres aux traits*, small drafting workshops supervised by architects. Parchment became cheaper and tracing techniques improved substantially; but despite these documents, it is still difficult to reconstruct the building process based solely on their details. The general practice was to draw plans of elevations and façades, never a complete structure. Lacking accuracy and uniformity of scale, they were more like summaries than technical prints for workers. Similarly, models made of wax or wood covered with plaster, held by saints or donors, can be seen in numerous paintings. They were a means of communication between architect and patron, not between architect and worker. Luckily there exists a document which provides a greater insight into the architect's workshop than all extant records and plans. It is the first and only known medieval textbook of architecture, a small encyclopedia of construction lore, a note-book of records and drawings, practical advice and inventions.

We are talking about the album of Villard de Honnecourt. Un-fortunately, the thirty-three preserved charts represent only half of the book. The entire section on wood construction and carpentry is missing, which was of crucial importance to the cathedral builders. Nevertheless the material contained in this architectural *vade mecum* overflows its pages.

Everything is there: mechanics, geometry and practical trigo-nometry, drawings of animals, people, ornaments and architectural details. Villard, who came from the small village of Honnecourt in Picardy, was a man of voracious curiosity. He travelled constantly and saw Gothic cathedrals in Meaux, Laon, Chartres, Reims; he ventured to Germany and Switzerland. He even reached Hungary and everywhere he drew and sketched things which attracted his attention: an outline of an organ loft, a grasshopper, a rosette, a lion, a human face emerging from the contour of a leaf, the descent from the Cross, nudes, figures in motion. Some drawings are schematic, written into an oblong or triangle as if Villard guided the heavy hand of a sculptor. Others, like a kneeling figure, surprise us with their finesse, ornamentation and the perfection with which he renders draperies. He was also interested in recent inventions: a saw which could be used underwater, a self-propelling wheel (the eternal dream of *perpetuum mobile*), and 'gadgets' — how to construct an angel always pointing his finger towards the sun, how to make a statue of an eagle turn its head towards a priest reading the Gospel, or a clever mechanism for warming a bishop's hands during a long mass.

Novelists present medieval architects as a sect which enviously guarded its secrets. If these secrets were truly important, they must have concerned pure science. If we accept this premise, architects in the Middle Ages would be the sole guardians of the properties of geom·trical figures, the principles of material resistance, as well as the basic laws of mechanics. Here Villard's notebook is silent. It is a collection of practical recipes, the cook-book of a medieval architect.

The history of science maintains that the knowledge of mathematics in the Middle Ages was limited. We have the corres-pondence between two scholars from the middle of the eleventh century: Ragimbold from Cologne and Radolf from Liège. A strict contemporary critic says that 'its analysis reveals ignorance'. The learned men are unable to conduct a simple geometrical proof and to calculate the external angle in a triangle. Who knows how long we would have had to wait for a new Euclid if it were not for the Arabs, who introduced Aristotle, Plato, Euclid and Ptolomey to Europe in the twelfth and thirteenth centuries. No doubt this knowledge graced the hands of architects. Yet it is by no means certain what use was made of it.

Our nineteenth-century grandparents were incorrigible optimists when they spoke about the rationalism of Gothic architecture. One is inclined towards those who claim that the knowledge of the cathedral builders was rather empirical, based on experiment and experience rather than calculation. Intuition invites error. Disasters during the construction of cathedrals were much more frequent than we might suppose, and did not stop at the famous accident in Beauvais or the ill-fated attempt to widen Siena's Duomo. A thorough investigation of Chartres' dome one hundred years after it was built, revealed a frightening state of affairs. The diagonal nave threatened to collapse, the portal had to be reinforced with iron bars. In the sixteenth century the condition of Notre-Dame was no less alarming. Why was it so? Usually the foundations were not strong enough for the spiralling constructions. The passion for height is well-illustrated by the altitude of naves built in consecutive order: Sens — thirty metres; Paris — thirty-two and a half; Chartres — about thirty-five metres; Bourges — thirty-seven metres; Reims — thirty-eight metres; Amiens — forty-two metres; and finally Beauvais — forty-eight metres.

The story of the construction of Milan Cathedral, which we know quite well through the records of a commission of experts, demonstrates something that should fill the rationalists with indignation. Let's imagine: the walls, already constructed, have reached a considerable height, yet the dispute is not over ornamental details but a quite fundamental matter — the plan of the cathedral. The French architect Jean Mignot violently criticizes his Italian colleagues, and utters the classical aphorism: '*Ars sine scientia nihil est*'. But this *scientia* belonged to the realm of empiricism, since none of the contending sides could produce a scholarly proof in defence of their convictions.

It is known that alchemy has more secrets than chemistry and that the branch of knowledge which surpasses all others in its esoteric character is the culinary art. The essential secret of medieval architects was the skill of building according to plans, but their knowledge incorporated thousands of kitchen secrets: the distinction of various kinds of stone, production of different mortars. The obligation to guard these secrets bound not only architects, but also stonemasons, stone-layers, plasterers, and those who mixed limestone mortars and dwelt on the lowest levels of the hierarchy. Similar principles governed other professions quite apart from architecture.

The real constitution of the cathedral builders are two manuscripts in English: one called 'Regius', written about 1390; and the other named 'Cook', older by forty years. Besides regulations governing religion, ethics and habits, they contain a separate law about discretion. They forbid the repetition of conversations held in lodges and other gatherings of stonemasons. For many years scholars thought that this interdiction concerned esoteric formulae and secrets. It referred however, as more recent research demonstrates, to specific technical and professional matters, like the manner of laying stones so that their position closely resembled their original place inside the rock from which they had been hewn.

For a long time it was believed that medieval builders communicated through secret signs. Recent research proves that this habit existed only in Scotland, connected with work in imported stone. It was, therefore, an ordinance protecting highly skilled craftsmen against the less knowledgeable, and only in certain locations.

The dispute whether cathedrals were built *more geometrico* or 'intuitively' like honeycombs, cannot be solved in general terms since the matter largely depended on the period, place and the current state of science, as well as on the education of a particular architect. Alexander Neckam, living at the end of the twelfth century, had the intuition of genius that the earth's gravitation is directed towards the centre of the globe. But his practical deduction from this principle was rather frightening, and it was fortunate that architects neglected to implement it. Neckam advised that walls should not be vertical, but should gradually fan outwards.

There is also the question of the module, an arbitrarily accepted measure whose product is repeated in different elements of the construction, like the length of the nave, the height of the columns, the proportion of the width of the transept to the main nave. There is no doubt that medieval architects used the module. An American archaeologist, Sumner Crosby, discovered that the module, quite consistantly employed, for Saint-Denis was 0.325 metres, which is approximately the length of the 'Paris Foot'. Yet it was not a principle of construction, but an aesthetic one. It was widely understood that the use of simple rules of geometry gave the harmony of proportions.

At first an architect was one of the artisans. He was paid daily and worked as a mason, and surprisingly, received even less pay than a stone-layer in Rouen, although he was given an annual bonus. In time the material rewards of the profession became more visible, as the daily wage was paid whether or not the architect was present at the site. To that we should add compensations in kind — clothing. In the beginning they were a sort of livery which stressed a relationship of servitude. But when we hear that in 1255 John Gloucester received a fur-lined coat, similar to those worn by the gentry, it is a clear sign of the ennoblement of the profession. The management, in order to bind the architect to his work, presented him with a horse, a house, and the honour of dining at the abbot's table. In Italy, even more so in England, the material situation of an architect was much better than in France. In the fourteenth century his annual income in the British Isles amounted to eighteen pounds — when twenty pounds of income from property could buy a nobleman's title. In the thirteenth century the court architect of Charles d'Anjou enjoyed the title of *proto-magister*, a troupe of house, and was counted amongst the knights.

The majority of Gothic cathedrals were the work of many architects. Nevertheless, attempts were made to entrust the supervision to one man for as long as possible. Life contracts were not unusual. They often included a clause which provided that in case of incurable illness, or the loss of sight, the architect would receive the agreed pension until the end of his days. In the late medieval period an architect often worked simultaneously on a number of constructions; but we can also find a draconian contract between the management of the Bordeaux Cathedral and Jean Lebas, who held the title of '*maçon, maître après Dieu des ouvrages des pierre*'. He was allowed to leave the construction site just once a year in order to visit his family. The possibility of travel was greatly desired by architects, since consultations were not only a supplementary and quite lucrative source of income, but also added to the craftsmen's prominence.

One should finally dispose of the myth of the cathedral builders' anonymity. Scores of their names were preserved, not only in chronicles and financial registers. The medieval constructors signed, if this is an appropriate term, their work with joy and pride.

In the cathedral of Chartres there is a design on the floor, which for a long time eluded the attention of scholars. It is a labyrinth shaped like a circle with a radius of eighteen metres, on which believers journeyed on their knees — an abbreviated version of the pilgrimage to the Holy Land. In the central part of this labyrinth, which is a distant echo of Cretan civilization, there was a commemorative plaque. Unfortunately none of the originals is preserved, though we have descriptions of two other inscriptions. They are not, as one might expect, a verse from the Gospel or a fragment of liturgical text. The inscription in the cathedral of Amiens was quite unexpected for those who held that medieval builders remained anonymous. It is written:

'In the year of 1220 of the Grace of Our Lord the construction of this church was begun. At that time the bishop was Evrart; the King of France was Louis, the son of Philip. He, who was the master of works was called Robert de Luzarches, and after him came Thomas de Cormont, and after him again his son Renaud, who placed the inscription in the year 1288.'

The figures of three architects in the company of the bishop were carved in white marble. Not only craftsmen passed on their names to posterity. The famous tympanum of Autun bears the inscription: '*Gislebertus fecit hoc opus*'. We also find signatures on architectural details, like capitals and keystones. On the keystone of the vault in Rouen Cathedral we read the proud statement: '*Durandus me fecit*'. Clement of Chartres has also signed his stained glass.

And finally, we come to signs on stone. The Middle Ages knew piece-work, but this system was most frequently used during the construction of castles, especially when executed by workers recruited by force. The walls of Aigues-Mortes are evidence. Such features are rarely found on cathedral stones and probably were made by new workers, whose abilities were not yet known to the supervisors. Very important were the quarry signs, especially when the material came from diverse sources. The general practice was to erect walls of identical or similar kinds of stone, which guaranteed endurance and allowed later renovations.

It is hard to imagine the precise orchestration of the crowds of sculptures populating the portals, eaves and galleries of cathedrals without a strict definition of their position. Mistakes happened of course. The symbols of the months in Notre-Dame are placed in reverse order. The builders of Reims wanted to avoid a similar error. Their cathedral was besieged by an army of three thousand sculptures. Therefore they carefully marked the positions of the sculptures on the walls.

The true signatures of the craftsmen appeared rather late. These were geometrical figures — triangles, polygons — occasionally pictures of tools like trowels, or letters of the alphabet. The signs were inherited; and if a father and son worked together, they added a small detail, for example, a dash to differentiate their stones. These signs, at first simple, gradually became more complex and inventive; and they were also used by the architects of the fifteenth century. Alexandre de Bernard placed a star-like pentagon at the end of his name. A modest sign carved on the stone, so that the builder was not deprived of his payment, became a signature and a symbol of professional pride.

The Hundred Years' War was a lethal blow to the art of cathedral building. But the first tokens of the crisis were visible earlier, at the end of the thirteenth century. The persecution of free thought swept through the continent: Roger Bacon died in prison in 1294; at the universities, liberty of speech was seriously curtailed. The centralizing power of the king, especially in France, snared city councils and subordinated them. Generous young bourgeois stopped contributing to the building of spires above which the dark clouds of war were gathering. The affair of the Templars is the symbolic end of an epoch.

Economic development was halted, population dropped, and inflation deepened. A charming song from 1313 informs us:

Il se peut que le roy nous enchante,
Premier nous fit vingt de soixante,
Puis de vingt, quatre et dix de trente.
. . . Or et argent tout est perdu,
Ne jamès n'en sera rendu.

The bankruptcy of the Italian Bank of Scala, registered by almost the whole of Europe, coincided with the outbreak of the Hundred Years' War. Religious architecture was replaced by military architecture. The time of thick walls had returned.

The construction sites of unfinished cathedrals stand desolate. No one is interested any longer in high arches and intricate vaults. The sons of those who sculpted an angel's smile turn cannon balls.

ALBIGENSIANS, INQUISITORS AND TROUBADOURS

TRAVELLING in the south of France, one now and again finds traces of the Albigensians. Inconspicuous traces — ruins, bones, a legend.

I witnessed a discussion during which learned professors were at each other's learned throats over the Albigensians. It is one of the most controversial questions in contemporary medieval studies. It may be worthwhile to take a closer look at this heresy, eradicated in the middle of the thirteenth century. Their story coincides with the ascendance of French power on the ruins of the duchy of Toulouse. The day when the stakes of Montségur burned was the day of the consolidation of the French empire. A flourishing civilization moving towards an important synthesis of oriental and occidental elements was destroyed at the very heart of Christian Europe. The obliteration from the religious map of the world of the Albigensian faith — which might have played as significant a role in the shaping of the human race's spirituality as Buddhism or Islam — is connected with the founding of a centuries-long institution called the Inquisition. It is no wonder that this knot of political, national and religious affiliations fans emotions and is so difficult to unravel.

Literature concerning the Albigensian question could fill a sizeable library. However, there are few original heretical texts, as frequently occurs in the history of culture. Not many works escape the sands and fires of history, thus human thought and suffering have to be reconstructed from dubious records and quotations in the writings of adversaries.

In order to understand the impact of the Albigensians, who flourished in the south of France between the eleventh and the

101

twelfth centuries, one should recall, at least briefly, their ancestry. There is no doubt that in their heresy, or — as others claim — religion, the voice of the Orient can be heard. Historians searching for the origins of this movement traced the following genealogy: the Gnostics (some reach as far back as Zoroaster), the Manichaeans, the Paulicians, the Bogomils — the Cathars (who in southern France were called the Albigensians, after the city of Albi). Their common characteristic was a sharp dualism, assuming the action of two principles in the universe, Good and Evil; and a belief that the material world was the work of the Devil (thus rejecting the Old Testament), which led to the extreme condemnation of flesh and matter, and to strict moral asceticism. The psychological background of these views was a fascination with the evil seen to be rampant, a fascination easy to explain in an epoch of crises, violence and wars.

The Gnostics have a rather bad reputation among many historians of philosophy, who would rather remove this chapter from their textbooks dedicated to the education of cool, analytical minds. Those who derive aesthetic satisfaction from intricate intellectual constructs, however, are always attracted to the theology of the Albigensians, their breathtaking ladder of hypostasis connecting heaven and earth.

A serious competitor with Christianity was Mani, a figure with exact dates of birth and death. He saw the sun in Babylonia, although he was Persian in origin, and was brought up among the Gnostics. A prophet of great influence at the royal court, convinced of his messianic mission, he travelled to India and later taught crowds of disciples. He died in twenty-six days of agony, chained to a rock by the Persian King Bahram. Discoveries in Turfan and Fayoum (sites thousands of kilometres apart) prove that he, who claimed to be the follower of Buddha, Zarathustra and Christ, tried to create a syncretic religion combining Buddhist, Mazdeic and Christian elements. The popularity of Mani's religion was immense, spreading through China, Central Asia, North Africa, Italy, Spain and Gaul.

The Manichaeans, through their wide influence, their prophet's martyrdom, their stress on dualism even stronger than the Gnostics' (the cosmic battle of the powers of Good and Evil was projected into the human soul, tearing it into two parts), constituted the main opposition to Christianity. The Church Fathers did not spare their anathemas, and the more philosophical ones engaged in polemics, like St Augustine (a renegade Manichaean) in his treatise *Contra Faustam*. He pushes his opponent to the wall trying to prove that the assumption of two principles of Good and Evil leads to polytheism. Faustus, however, parries the dialectical thrusts. 'It is true that we assume two principles, but only one of them we call God, the other we call *hyle*, or matter, or else the Demon. If you claim that such practice is tantamount to worship of two gods, you must also claim that a doctor, whose concern is health and illness, creates two notions of health.' After the arguments spoke the sword, and Manichaeism was drowned in a sea of blood in the fourth century. Only in China did it survive, until the thirteenth century and the invasion of Genghis Khan.

The story of the Paulicians, a dualist sect in Armenia, on the border of Persia and Byzantium, which created a state or rather half a sovereign colony, is a fascinating episode in world history. The Catholic Bishop of Armenia accused them of worshipping the sun, a typically Manichaean feature; but the Paulicians always stressed their adherence to Christianity, probably for political reasons. Their small but stalwart army reached the Bosphorus, and was only defeated by Basil I during the battle of Bartyrhax in 872. For his time, Basil's treatment of the defeated was humane; they were deported to the Balkans — a meaningful detail, as we shall see later.

It is questionable to what degree these heretical sects were conscious of belonging to the same tradition of religious thought. But here we reach a point at which their interrelationship becomes quite clear. In the tenth century the Bogomils appear in Bulgaria. They preach dualism with even greater fervour than the Paulicians, claiming that the empirical world is the creation of Satan and that man — a mixture of water and earth — has a soul created by the breath of both Satan and God. The Bogomils oppose both Rome and Byzantium. They engage in intense proselytizing and reach the Apennine Peninsula, Tuscany and Lombardy, as well as the south of France. Here they find receptive ground, giving birth to the powerful Cathar heresy (after the Greek word meaning 'pure'), who call themselves the Patarini in Bosnia and Dalmatia, and the Albigensians in France.

The sources are scarce. I shall enumerate the primary ones. First, *Interrogatio Johannis* (or 'The Secret Supper of John the Evangelist'), an apocryphal document from the thirteenth century 'falsifying', as an inquisitor notes, the Gospel of St John. Its subject is a conversation between John and Christ in heaven concerning such problems as the fall of Satan, his rule, the Creation, Christ's descent to earth and the Last Judgement. This unusually beautiful text pre-dates the Latin writings of the Cathars, and clearly points to Bogomil ancestry. Two versions have been preserved: the so-called Carcassonne version, which can be found in an outstanding collection of documents called *Collection Doat*, and the Vienna version.

The only extant theological work of the Cathars is the *Liber de duobus principiis* from the end of the thirteenth century. The text is far from a coherent scholastic discourse divided into chapters and paragraphs. Its most interesting section is on free will, important from a doctrinal point of view, as well as its sections on cosmogony and polemics. The latter proves that Catharism, by no means a uniform movement, was divided into schools and at least two factions: the mitigated and the absolute dualists. The author of the treatise (scholars believe it was an Italian, Giovanni di Lugio) represents the absolutist position, which claims that Evil is as eternal as Good, and that ontological being and nothingness — also understood as cosmic powers — always existed. One should stress, however, that polemics between the Cathars were like family quarrels; opponents never reached for anathema as an ultimate weapon.

Finally *The Ritual of the Cathars*, a liturgical treatise which has reached us in two versions: the Lyon version in *langue d'oc* and the Florentine version in Latin. Historians of religion sometimes pay inadequate atttention to the problems of rituals, yet it is in ritual, and not in theological concepts, that the degree of spiritualization of a religion finds its fullest expression. The Cathar liturgy is striking for it austerity and simplicity. They rejected most sacraments, for example marriage, as a consequence of their negative attitude toward matters of the flesh. But they accepted what today would be called civil marriage; hence the inquisitors' registers frequently record the word *amasia*, which means concubine, referring to a Cathar's wife. There was common confession, and the most important sacrament was the *consolamentum*: spiritual baptism granted only to adults after a long period of preparation, prayer and fasting. The recipient left the flock of 'believers' to join the exclusive, pre-determined élite of the 'perfected'.

The ritual was held in a private house. The white-washed walls were without ornament. There were some simple pieces of furniture and a table covered with a snow-white cloth, the Gospel and lighted candles. A candidate for perfection renounced the Catholic creed, promised not to eat meat or any animal products, not to kill, never to swear, and to avoid all carnal relations. He donated his property to the Cathar Church. From then on he devoted himself totally to apostolic work and charitable acts, especially tending to the sick, a paradox among people treating the body with contempt. He also swore never to renounce his creed, and history records only three names of the perfected who were daunted by the stake.

We look in vain for traces of magic, initiation rites or gnosis in Cathar ritual. It referred rather, as Dondaine accurately observes, to the rites of earliest Christianity.

A summary of Cathar doctrine would require a complete system of subtle theological notions, beyond the scope of this essay, which is limited to the basic facts.

René Nelli, a publisher, translator and commentator on Cathar texts, claims that the basic difference between Catharism and Catholicism consisted in the fact that for the Roman Church, evil was a punishment for sins and in a sense remained at God's disposal, while for the Cathars, God suffered from evil but did not inflict punishment. The empirical world was the work of Satan, the first-born, fallen son of God. So was man, an alliance of being with nothingness. Hell did not exist; there were, however, reincarnations in which individuals would lose their carnality, ascending toward the light or sinking into evil matter. The Cathars rejected the Old Testament (the God of Moses was synonymous with the Devil) and considered the Gospel the only book worth reading and reflection. Yet Christ was not God incarnate, but an emanation of the Highest One. Because He was an incorporeal being, He could not suffer. The Cathars rejected the symbolism of the Cross as a brutal materialization of spiritual matters. They considered the Catholic Church a satanic institution, the 'whore of Babylon'. The end of the world would come in a cosmic conflagration: souls would return to God and matter would be destroyed. The consequence of this eschatology was the assumption that everyone would be saved after an appropriately long chain of incarnations — the only optimistic feature of this severe heresy.

Was it a heresy? In his book *Montségur*, Fernand Niel advances a daring yet plausible thesis: the Cathars were not heretics but founders of a new religion, utterly divorced from Roman Catholicism. If we accept this argument, the Albigensian crusade appears in a different light, and the moral motives of the crusaders would be seriously called into question.

The author of this sketch is not a professional historian, but a story-teller. It frees him from the bond of scholarly objectivity, allows the play of prejudice and passion, from which even scholars are not entirely free. It is enough to compare two prominent works on the Albigensian crusade, one by Professor Pierre Belperron, the other by Zoë Oldenbourg: both rely on primary sources, and reach completely opposite conclusions. Not only those who act in history, but also those who write about it, feel the presence of the black demon of intolerance behind their backs.

We shall provide some justification by talking about the defeated.

In March 1208, Pope Innocent III proclaimed a crusade against Raymond VI, the Christian Count of Toulouse — a cousin of the King of France, brother-in-law of the kings of England and Aragon, one of the greatest rulers in Europe. His vast realm, including Provence and stretching to the Pyrenees in the south, was powerful not only due to alliances and feudal relations. Its numerous, rich cities were heirs to the spirit of liberty and the old Mediterranean civilization. They were ruled by Roman Law, and their elected governments — city councils and consuls — were the true rulers. The largest were autonomous republics with their own judiciaries, with privileges long undreamt of by the cities of the north. An atmosphere of freedom and equality reigned in these communities, without religious or racial prejudice. Arab doctors were held in high esteem, and Jews often participated in the city councils. Prominent schools of medicine, philosophy, astronomy and mathematics functioned long before the foundation of universities, and not only in the capital — the 'pink city' of Toulouse, the third city of Europe after Rome and Venice — but also in centres such as Narbonne, Avignon, Montpellier, Béziers. It was in Toulouse, not Paris, that Aristotle's philosophy, rediscovered by the Arabs, was first taught. The cast of mind in these regions resembles that in the Renaissance, whose beginnings were here, not in Italy. The language of the south of France — the *langue d'oc* — was the language of European poetry in the twelfth and thirteenth centuries, until conquest reduced it to the rank of a dialect. Poets from Germany, England, France, Italy and Catalonia arduously imitated the great lyrical works of the troubadours. Even Dante originally intended writing his *Divine Comedy* in *langue d'oc*.

If we can identify a single word which would be the key to a dead civilization, like *kalos kagathos* for the Greeks, and *virtus* for the Romans, such a word for the South would be *paratge*, declined innumerable times in the troubadours' poems, and meaning honour, integrity, equality, condemnation of brute force, and respect for individuals.

Thus one might say that in the south of France there existed a separate civilization, and that the Albigensian crusade was a clash of two cultures. The defeat of the duchy of Toulouse is one of the catastrophes of humanity, like the destruction of Cretan or Mayan civilizations.

The paradox of this civilization consisted in the co-existence of an epicurean lifestyle and passionate love poetry, with the veneration of the Cathars, who offended the Church with their excessive asceticism. To solve this mystery, scholars suggest that the Lady in the poetry of the troubadours is the symbol of the Cathar Church. A risky thesis. Nevertheless, research has proved that some trouba-dours were influenced by the heresy (and by mystical Arabian poetry), and that they understood love not as physical passion, but as a method of achieving spiritual and moral perfection.★

Languedoc, with Lombardy and Bulgaria, was one of the European countries most affected by the Cathar heresy, whose followers came from all social strata, from peasants to princes. The roots of the popularity of the new religion can be traced to the corruption of the Catholic Church in southern France, to a specific intellectual and emotional situation, and simply to the attractiveness of Catharism. Around 1167 a meeting of Albigensians was held in St-Félix-de-Caraman, under the leadership of Nicestas, the chief missionary from Constantinople, establishing the organization and ritual of the southern Cathar Church.

Naturally the Roman Church felt threatened by the spread of the heresy. One must admit that the first attempts to regain control were through peaceful, intellectual means: joint debates with the Cathars about dogma, missions by prominent preachers such as St Bernard

---

★ Jaufré Rudel writes: '. . . I have a friend, but I do not know who she is, and, for my soul, I have never seen her . . . although I love her so much. There is no greater happiness for me, than to possess a remote love.'

of Clairvaux, which ended in failure due to open hostility towards the Church. 'The basilicas are without the faithful, the faithful without priests, priests without respect.'

The situation changed when the papal throne fell to thirty-seven-year-old Lotario Conti, who took the name of Innocent III. His face in a fresco in the church of Subiaco emanates peace and strength; but his spiritual rule in Languedoc was ill-judged, to put it mildly, partly because of the inertia of the local clergy, partly because of the officious papal legates. Though morally responsible for the Albigensian crusade, the new Pope was by no means a religious fanatic; his letters, even taking into account official style, are concerned with justice and are moderate in tone.

The same cannot be said of his envoy — a Cistercian monk, Pierre de Castelnau, who with Ralph de Fontfroide went to Languedoc charged with suppressing the heresy. He seems to have been a fanatic lacking any political sense, diplomatic talents, or even the simplest tact. Nominated as the Pope's envoy with special powers, he took as his assistant Arnaud Aimery, Abbot of Cîteaux. Their actions produced a chain of misunderstanding and embitterment. Of equally little effect were the arduous sermons of St Dominic, who received instead of the crown of martyrdom ('I beg you not to kill me instantly, but to sever my limbs one by one') laughter and mockery. The continuous debating, being a clash of two separate worlds, traditions and mentalities, had few results. Defenders of the Catholic faith sometimes lost patience, as exemplified by St Bernard of Verfeil — 'Let God curse you, thick-skinned heretics, among whom I sought more subtle intelligence in vain' — or Brother Etienne de Minia, who tried to exclude from philosophical disputes Esclarmonde, the sister of the Count of Foix: 'Go attend to your spinning-wheel, Lady; it does not become you to have a voice in these matters.'

Finally Pierre de Castelnau reached the conclusion that only force could suppress the heresy. Unable to arrange a coalition of Provençal lords under the leadership of Raymond VI, he pronounced anathema on the Count of Toulouse. 'He who would disinherit you will be in the right, and he who would kill you will be blessed.' Such was the conclusion of the mission of the papal emissary who, having nothing more to do, was returning to Rome.

He was murdered by an assassin in Saint-Gilles, on the morning of 15 January 1208. Raymond's men became the main suspects. The martyr's blood-stained shirt was carried from castle to castle, and the faithful were summoned to a crusade. Raymond VI, seeing the danger, decided to submit to the Pope's will. In June 1209, accompanied by three archbishops, nineteen bishops, dignitaries, vassals, clergy and laity, with bare chest and a rope around his neck, flogged with rods, he walked to the stone lions guarding the portal of the beautiful cathedral in Saint-Gilles. The treaty signed after this ceremony surrendered the duchy to the Church. Moreover, Raymond surprised everyone by taking the Cross and joining the army of crusaders taking rafts down the Rhône.

The mighty train of men, horses and iron dragging itself along is terrifying to see. Among the army are Flemish, Normans, Burgundians, French and Germans. They are led by bishops, archbishops, Duke Odo of Burgundy, the counts of Nevers, Boulogne, and Saint-Pol, renowned barons and knights like Simon de Montfort and Guy de Lévis. The rest of the force is composed of sergeants, foot-soldiers and mercenaries — a ruthless mob known to every medieval army, composed of cut-throats hungry for blood and spoils. The most highly-priced hirelings come from the Basque, Aragonese and Brabant regions. They are lowly types in the military hierarchy, but often a decisive factor in battle. If we add auxiliary units and crowds of pilgrims lured by the possibility of pious contemplation of burning stakes, the figure of three hundred thousand provided by chronicles does not sound exaggerated, assuming that the army of knights was but a small fraction of this mass, like the percentage of tanks to infantry in a modern army.

The first of the nobles to meet the crusaders' swords is the Viscount of Carcassonne, Béziers and Albi, twenty-five-year-old Raymond-Roger from the Trencavel family. Frightened by the advance of the enemy army, he attempts to negotiate with the Pope's legate. In vain. The heavy war machine, 'an army never seen before', cannot be stopped once put in motion. Raymond-Roger barricades himself in Carcassonne, while the crusaders follow the old Roman road towards Béziers.

The town is situated on a hill over the Orb River. It has solid walls and sufficient food. The Bishop of Béziers tries to negotiate, but the crusaders present a list of two hundred and twenty persons accused of heresy, and demand their surrender. The town councillors answer with dignity that they prefer to be 'drowned in the salty sea' than to deliver their citizens. The siege begins. On Ste Marie-Madeleine's day, 22 July, before military action commences, matters take a tragic turn for the defenders. A group of burghers, encouraged by the passivity of the huge army, leaves the city walls with 'great white banners, and runs forward until out of breath, hoping to flush the enemy away, like a flock of sparrows from a stand of oats'. 'Immense imprudence', because the army of mercenaries immediately leaps to its feet.

They are barefooted, armed with clubs and knives, dressed only in shirts and trousers, but their thirst for blood is inexhaustible. They manage to break into the town following the members of the careless expedition. Once inside, they spread terror; the assault on the walls takes only a few hours. A crowd of survivors gathers in Saint-Nazaire Cathedral, and in the churches of La Madeleine and Sainte-Jude. The soldiery break down the doors and slaughter everyone: the new-born, women, cripples, elders, and priests celebrating mass. Bells toll for the dead. Extermination is total.

Pierre de Vaux-de-Cernay, a Cistercian monk and chronicler of the expedition against the Albigensians, wrote that in La Madeleine alone seven thousand were slaughtered, which is probably an exaggeration. Historians estimate, however, that some thirteen thousand 'innocent' people were killed in Béziers. What makes this figure even more terrifying is that inhabitants were put to the sword without discrimination. The papal legate, Arnaud Aimery, when asked during the battle what was to be done with the Catholics who must have been among those massacred, said: 'Kill everyone. God will recognize his own.' This famous response is probably apocryphal, since it is quoted by a fourteenth-century chronicler, Caesarius of Heisterbach. It is likely that Arnaud Aimery — a blockhead rather than a cynic — uttered only the first sentence. Nevertheless, this dictum provides a perfect commentary on the events.

As a result of the quarrel between the mercenaries and the regular army over the division of spoils, the town was set on fire 'together with the cathedral built by Master Gervaise, which broke in half with a rumble in the heat of the flames, and fell in two.' With flying banners the crusaders turned towards the walls of Carcassonne, a city of thirty spires sheltering Viscount Raymond-Roger.

The Carcassonne of today, reconstructed by Viollet-le-Duc, gives only a faint notion of what this fortress was, surrounded by a double wall. The first feature which strikes a visitor is the small space between the walls, about ten thousand square metres. In August

1209 the city gave asylum to tens of thousands of people, not counting cattle and horses. Despite that, the battle was fierce, and young Raymond-Roger conducted it with the talent and bravura of an experienced commander. The hot summer became an ally of the crusaders. A dark cloud of flies and the odour of pestilence hung over Carcassonne. Lack of water forced the defenders to capitulate after a fortnight's siege.

The events that followed provoke controversies among scholars, and the reports of Guillaume de Tudèle and Guillaume de Puylaurent are full of insinuations, but do not cast enough light on this significant episode. No agreement is signed between the crusaders and Raymond-Roger, and worse still, in a violation of the knightly code, the Viscount is imprisoned, soon dying of dysentery. The Pope's envoy presses for the election of his successor from among the senior French crusaders, in contravention of feudal law, especially as Raymond-Roger's four-year-old son is alive. Magnanimously, the French lords and counts refuse the title and inheritance after his tragic death. 'There was no one who would not feel it was a loss of honour to accept the land,' says Guillaume de Tudèle.

Then enters a man whose figure would cast an ominous shadow on Provence and Languedoc for many years: Simon de Montfort. He has long been remembered as a warrior who, accompanied by a handful of loyal men, could shake the foundations of an empire. He was a prototype conquistador — a fanatic, whose horizons were limited by his military helmet, a man with a strong arm, ambitious, energetic, exceedingly talented as a commander: a perfect candidate to be Viscount of Carcassonne and Béziers. In addition, he had distinguished himself in the Fourth Crusade and was a direct vassal of the King of France.

The fall of Carcassonne opened the gates of many castles for de Montfort, but the forty days for which the crusaders were pledged to fight the heretics came to an end, and the warriors departed north. Simon de Montfort remained, with a contingent of about thirty knights. Of course during the eight years of constant struggle 'the lion of the crusades' received reinforcements. The country was terrorized, but by no means conquered.

In June 1210, de Montfort besieged Minèrve, a city situated between Carcassonne and Béziers among deep gorges and a deserted countryside. The fortress was defended bravely, but a siege-machine destroyed the castle's water supply system, and the defenders were forced to negotiate. According to accepted practice, heretics who renounced their faith would be spared. One of de Montfort's captains, Robert de Mauvoisin, protested. He had come to destroy heresy, not to show indulgence. Arnaud Aimery consoled him: 'Rest assured, sir, few will be converted.' He was right. The first great stake in the conquered city consumed one hundred and fifty men and women, who 'died with courage worthy of a better cause', commented sadly the Benedictine Dom Vaissete.

Actually the war had long stopped being an expedition against heretics, and had become a great battle between the North and the South, a war of nations; however many castles de Montfort captured, the country was not conquered. Noblemen waited in their eagles' nests for the right moment, towns rebelled, and French garrisons placed in captured fortresses were often reduced to one man. Sieges grew harder and harder. Béziers fell after a few hours; it took fifteen days to conquer Carcassonne, and Minèrve only surrendered after six weeks.

The fortress of Termes was besieged by the crusaders for four months. The castle's position was perfect. In order to approach it, one had to 'jump into an abyss, then crawl towards the sky'. The army besieging Termes was demoralized, reduced to half its original size, and starved. After three difficult months of siege the bishops accompanying de Montfort wanted to leave him. On the evening of the next day, the commander of the fortress declared his willingness to negotiate. The cisterns in the town had dried up; once again water proved the crusaders' ally. But at night there was a downpour, and Raymond, the leader of the garrison, shut himself up in the fortress. The ensuing battle was fierce and dramatic. De Montfort's chaplain was killed during mass, and his closest companion, with whom he used to walk arm-in-arm, was beheaded by a stone-throwing machine. De Montfort was resigned. He contemplated ending the siege and joining a monastery. One day the fortress fell silent, and the crusaders discovered to their amazement that it was empty. This time rats defeated the besieged: during the dry weather they got into the cisterns and poisoned the water.

The war draws closer to the duchy of Toulouse and the county of Foix. According to a methodical plan of conquest, the crusaders besiege Lavaur. It is defended by Aimery de Montréal, a former ally of de Montfort and a son of Blanche de Laurac, a famous 'perfected one'. The lady is also known for her loyalty to the Cathar Church and her charitable works. The walls of Lavaur fall after a heroic defence lasting over two months. The commander and eighty knights are hanged. A hastily-built scaffold collapses under their weight, and henchmen have to finish off victims by cutting their throats. The Countess is thrown into a well and stoned. A gigantic stake, the largest of the war, devours four hundred Albigensians, who step into the flames singing *cum ingenio gaudio.*

The inevitable confrontation with the Count of Toulouse draws nearer, since the crusaders have no doubt that Raymond is an unreliable ally. The latter does everything to save his lands from war, but the pressure of the Pope's legate cannot be resisted. De Montfort besieges the heart of the country, the capital of Languedoc, Toulouse; but suddenly he himself is besieged at Castelnaudary. A bloody yet indecisive battle is fought under the town walls.

De Montfort's ambitions disturb the Pope, who suspends the crusade and grants the title of Duke of Narbonne to his envoy, Arnaud Aimery — thus starting a lasting feud between two men who had so far worked hand-in-hand.

At this point the King of Aragon enters the war game: Pedro II, connected by feudal ties with Languedoc, brother-in-law of the Count of Toulouse, and former leader of the crusade against the Spanish Moslems, the conqueror from Las Navas de Tolosa. For some time, though to little avail, he had tried to play the role of mediator between his neighbours and the French; now, relying on his military glory, he attempts to explain to the Pope that a war against heretics has turned into a barbarian conquest and colonization of a Christian country.

When his arguments yield no result, Pedro II with the finest knights of Aragon and Catalonia crosses the Pyrenees in September 1213, and joins Raymond VI. The proportion of knights is 900 to 2000, to de Montfort's disadvantage, when both armies prepare for battle near the town of Muret. In a council of war, Raymond proposes to wait for an assault, then to counter-attack and push the enemy towards the castle, where it would soon have to capitulate. This sane plan seems insufficiently picturesque and knightly to the Spaniards. Meanwhile de Montfort falls upon the Aragonese with Napoleonic speed and bravura, as the armies clash in a deadly embrace. 'It sounded as though a huge forest were falling under axe-blows.' Pedro II, a thirty-nine-year-old warrior with the strength of a tiger, does not command the fight, but is in the centre of

113

the chaos which constituted medieval battles. After a fierce fight he is killed; news of their king's death spreads panic among the army. A sudden attack by de Montfort on their flanks disperses his enemies, among them the Count of Toulouse's army, which did not even have the opportunity to take part in the battle. The infantry of Languedoc, while storming the walls of Muret, is decimated; up to twenty thousand men disappear in the quick current of the Garonne. Half a year later, without losing a single soldier, de Montfort enters Toulouse, the Rome of the Cathars. Raymond VI and his son seek asylum at the court of the King of England.

De Montfort becomes the ruler of a country larger than the domain of the King of France. The fate of Languedoc seems to be sealed, but in effect the leader has only as much land as French soldiers are able to defend.

On 16 July 1216, Pope Innocent III dies, and nineteen-year-old Raymond VII lands in Marseille, to an enthusiastic welcome. He immediately besieges Beaucaire and forces Simon de Montfort's brother to surrender. The inhabitants of Toulouse build barricades and chase away the French. Raymond VI, marching through the Pyrenees with an Aragonese army, enters his capital, welcomed with tears of joy. Defeated for the first time, de Montfort besieges the city in vain, despite reinforcements. The humiliated 'lion of the crusades' is a different man now, and a cardinal-legate, Bertrand, complains that the great warrior is stricken with a sudden inertia, 'asking God only to give him peace and to relieve him by death from so many sufferings'. In the ninth month of the siege, during a morning raid by the Toulousians, Simon's brother, Guy de Montfort is wounded. As the commander runs from a tent where he has been hearing mass, a huge stone from a catapult strikes the Count's helmet, 'so mighty a blow it crushed his eyes and his brain, his teeth, his brow and his jaws. And the Count fell to the ground, dead, bloodied, and pallid.'

> *Montfort*
> *es mort*
> *es mort*
> *es mort*
> *viva Toloza*
> *ciotat gloriosa*
> *et poderosa*
> *tornan lo paratge et l'onor!*

This cry of joy could be heard from the Alps to the Ocean.

Simon's son Amaury is but a shadow of his talented father. Twice defeated, he delivers the conquered lands to the King of France. The old order returns to Languedoc. On 15 January 1224 Amaury de Montfort leaves Carcassonne forever, with his father's huge body sewn into a bull's hide.

After this first act came the expedition of Louis VIII, the work of his ambitious wife, Blanche de Castile, trying by any means to stop the agreement between Raymond VI and the Pope. Despite the heroic defence of Avignon, the new war was a military walk-over; but the army was harassed by pestilence, and King Louis VIII died on his way back. A new royal governor-general in Carcassonne, Humbert de Beaujeu, energetically continued the work of de Montfort, reclaiming the lost castles and introducing a new weapon against the recalcitrant country. 'In the morning, after mass and breakfast,' says the historian Guillaume de Puylaurent, 'the crusaders set off preceded by archers . . . and started to destroy the vineyards situated closest to the city, while its inhabitants slept; later they retreated to the nearby fields, destroying everything as they went.' The environs of unconquered Toulouse and other cities were turned into a desert. The war of castles continued.

In his *History of the Albigensians*, Napoléon Peyrat estimates the losses of the South during the fifteen years of war to be one million dead. Other scholars consider this figure excessive, yet all admit a tremendous loss of blood. The chronicles, as always, describe the deaths of knights and heroes, but true to Homeric tradition they are indifferent to the mounds of anonymous victims.

Only deadly exhaustion and the prospect of his country's complete ruin can explain why Raymond VII, the conqueror of de Montfort and defier of the King of France, signed in 1229 a treaty in Meaux, agreeing to conditions of the kind usually imposed on a vanquished enemy. The sovereign of Languedoc pledged not only loyalty to the Church and the King of France, but also committed himself to fighting against the 'infidel'. Especially severe was the obligation to pay two marks to anyone apprehending a heretic. It was also declared that the fortifications of Toulouse, along with thirty other castles, would be demolished, and the majority of fortresses handed over to the King of France. New borders were drawn, and of the old territory only one-third remained. Raymond VII gave his daughter as wife to the brother of Louis IX, Alphonse de

Poitiers, and since the Count of Toulouse had no son, this move sealed the fate of Languedoc.

The celebration of the signing of the treaty was held in the newly-built cathedral of Notre-Dame on Maundy Thursday 1229. With their victory over the German Emperor at Bouvines, the Capetians started to believe in their mission. The ceremony was clearly aimed at humiliating de Montfort's conqueror, and was held in the presence of the young King Louis IX, the Queen, prelates and the citizens of Paris. Raymond VII, dressed only in a shirt and with a rope round his neck, was led by the legates of Poland and England to the altar, where a cardinal-legate awaited him with a rod. 'It was a pity to see this great Duke,' writes Guillaume de Puylaurent, 'who had resisted the power of so many nations for so long, being led barefoot . . . to the steps of the altar.' Tradition holds that kneeling in front of the prelate, the Duke burst into mad laughter. Perhaps he thought then of how his father had been scourged at Saint-Gilles, twenty years before. When he returned to Toulouse, the commissars of the Church and the King were already at work, governing the land that they had failed to win in battle. Troubadour Sicard de Marvejols complains:

Ai Toloza et Provensa
e la terra d'Argensa
Bezers et Carcassey
Quo vos vi quo vos vei.

The new papal legate, Cardinal Romanus of St Angelo, a councillor and one of the instigators of the Treaty of Meaux, convened a synod in Toulouse to outline the methods of struggle with the Albigensians. Forty-five articles for tracking down, examining and punishing heretics were established. Thus the Inquisition was born, which proved to be a more effective weapon than the crusaders' swords; its development and influence on future institutions vastly exceeded the events described in this essay.

The *Capitula* established by the synod in Toulouse are worth quoting, at least in part:

'In each parish bishops will appoint one priest and three — or more, if necessary — laymen of impeccable reputation, who will swear to search for heretics in their parish with perseverance and faith. They will meticulously search all suspicious houses, rooms and cellars, and even the most secret corners. Upon finding heretics, or people giving them support, shelter or aid, they should undertake appropriate measures to prevent their escape, and also notify the bishop, the lord or his representative.

'The lords should search carefully for the heretics in towns, houses and forests, look for their meeting places and destroy their shelters.

'Whosoever lets a heretic remain on his land — for money or other reason — will lose his land in perpetuity, and will be punished by the lord according to his guilt.

'Also he on whose land heretics frequently meet will be punished, even if it were without his knowledge, but through his neglect.

'A house in which a heretic is found will be destroyed, and the land confiscated.

'A lord's deputy, who does not search the places suspected of being heretical meeting-places with sufficient ardour, will lose his position without redress.

Everybody has the right to search for heretics on his neighbour's land . . . Also the King can chase them on the land of the Count of Toulouse, and vice versa.

'*Hereticus vestitus*, he who renounces his heresy spontaneously cannot remain in the place of habitation considered to be affected by heresy. He will be moved to a place known as Catholic. The converted will wear two crosses on their clothes — one on the right, one on the left side — of a different colour from their clothes. They will not be able to hold public office, or perform legal acts until their rehabilitation is notified by the Pope or his legate, after an appropriate punishment.

'A heretic who seeks to return to the Catholic community not out of conviction, but out of fear of death or some other reason, will be placed in prison by the bishop, and held there with all precautions against his spreading his heresy to others.

'All adult Catholics will take an oath in front of their bishop to keep their creed, and to track down heretics with all the means at their disposal. This oath is to be renewed every two years.

'He who is suspected of heresy cannot be a doctor. If a sick person receives the Holy Communion from his vicar, he should be watched carefully, so that no heretic or person suspected of heresy gains access to him, since such visits have sad consequences.'

At first the Inquisition was the domain of bishops and local clergy, but the clergy proved too slow in putting the cruel machinery into motion. In 1233 Pope Gregory IX gave the Dominicans inquisitiorial powers. They were responsible only to the Pope; their sentences could be quashed only by him, which was a change of fundamental significance giving the Inquisition autonomous power, with immense prerogatives.

The legal acts that followed made the synod's decisions in Toulouse even stricter. The articles of the synod of Arles, for example, provide for the bodies of dead heretics to be exhumed and burned at the stake. A wave of false conversions forces the inquisitors to use increasingly severe measures. Prisons are built to house for life all those who simulate conversion. In 1243 a meeting in Narbonne decides that no one can be released from prison because of family obligations, age or poor health. The ruling to keep the names of prosecution witnesses secret is an obvious violation of Roman Law. The testimony of criminals, the infamous, and criminal conspirators is approved in cases of heresy. Even the testimony of people openly hostile to a defendant, or those whose only motive is vindictive, is not over-ruled as evidence.

History preserves the names of the first two inquisitors: Pierre Seila, son of a rich burgher of Toulouse and one of the first Dominicans, and Guillaume Arnaud, from Montpellier. Both were determined to dispatch their duties with great energy. Soon after their nomination they imprisoned and executed Vigoros de la Bacone, the alleged leader of the heretics in Toulouse. Guillaume Arnaud travelled the provinces, carrying out measures which terrified the people and alarmed the Count. Raymond complained to the Pope about the inquisitors' illegal procedures: examining witnesses behind closed doors, refusing defendants legal assistance, putting the dead on trial, and spreading such fear that the terrified citizens denounced the innocent. 'They upset the country, and because of their abuses the population turns against monks and clergy.'

It may be thought that the inquisitors commanded great resources. In fact the two Dominicans had neither means nor people of their own, and had to depend entirely on the assistance of the clergy and lay authorities. Only later did they receive permission for armed guards, tribunal assistants, notaries, assessors, though the number of personnel could not exceed eighty per inquisitor. Thus the development of the institution can be explained only by immense energy, a sense of mission, and the temptation of martyrdom.

Among the many works of art devoted to the struggle of the Dominicans against heresy, one of the most striking is the fresco by

Andrea da Firenze in the Spanish Chapel in Santa Maria Novella in Florence. Preaching brothers convert the heretics, who in shame tear up their godless books. Yet it is a euphemistic version of history. The truth is depicted at the bottom of the painting, disguised in animal symbolism: dogs, *Domini canes*, tearing up wolves — the heretics.

The cast of mind at that time is well illustrated by the affair of Jean Textor. He lived on the outskirts of Toulouse, and was most probably a Catholic. He addressed people in a frightened manner: 'Gentlemen, listen to me! I am not a heretic, for I have a wife and I sleep with her, I have sons, I eat meat, and I lie and swear, and I am a faithful Christian. So don't let them say these things about me, for I truly believe in God. They can accuse you as well as me. Look out for yourselves; wicked men want to ruin the town and honest men and to take the town away from its lord.' Despite the indignation of the people of Toulouse, Textor was imprisoned and eventually burned at the stake.

The number of suspects was so great that Arnaud and Seila were not able to examine all those arrested. Those sentenced to carrying a cross, to a fine or a pilgrimage, lived in uncertainty, because the only definitive sentence was that of death. But even the dead could not rest in peace. Cemeteries were full of open graves, from which bodies were exhumed to be purified by fire. The cruelty of the Dominicans was so extreme that it evoked the indignation of other orders. The monks of Belleperche gave shelter to heretics in their monastery, which was certainly not an isolated case.

In his *Chronicle*, Guillaume Pelhisson tells a story which would seem the tale of a madman full of sound and fury, were it not that the chronicler was an eye-witness, and as the inquisitors' assistant cannot be suspected of denigrating his masters. On 4 August 1234, after celebrating mass, Raymond de Miramont, the Bishop of Toulouse, was informed that in a nearby home an old woman had received the *consolamentum*. The Bishop, accompanied by priests, went to the home of the dying lady who, unaware of the situation and convinced that her visitor was a Cathar bishop, proclaimed her beliefs. Called to convert to Catholicism, she refused, upon which she was transported on her bed to a hastily built stake, and burned. Having fulfilled their task, the Bishop and his train returned to the refectory, 'and, giving thanks to God and the Blessed Dominic, ate with rejoicing what had been prepared for them'.

Such practices provoked riots in the city, which reached their apogee when the inquisitors indicted two city councillors accused of supporting heretics; in fact the lay authorities did all they could to save sentenced citizens, or to allow their escape. As the result of an open confrontation, the Dominicans were expelled and Bishop Raymond left Toulouse. But after an exchange of violent letters between the Duke and the Pope, they returned, and it started all over again. One of the perfected, a Catholic convert, denounced a number of important people, resulting in a series of posthumous trials. Cemeteries were ploughed up, and mortal remains were nailed to fences amidst cries of '*Qui atal fara, atal pendra*'.

In 1233 the first inquisitor to be martyred fell under the assault of a mob in Cordes; then acts of resistance multiplied. In addition, fights between groups of Catholics and heretics broke out in once peaceful towns.

It would be unfair to claim that all those caught in the brothers' net went to the stake. Documents record that a considerable number were pardoned. In 1241 during one week, two hundred and forty-one people received canonical absolution. The protocols of interrogations, however, were the basis of very precise files, and of the terrifying rumour 'they know everything'. History — not only of the Middle Ages — teaches that a nation subjected to police measures is demoralized, crumbles from within and loses its ability to resist. Even the most ruthless hand-to-hand combat is less disastrous than whispers, informing, a fear of one's neighbour and the scent of betrayal.

It is worth comparing the criminal procedure of the period with the procedure of the Inquisition. The Code of Justinian, on which criminal law was based, gave the defendant several rights, burdened the prosecution with the task of collecting proof, excluded witnesses whose impartiality was doubtful, and also required that the denouncer confront the defendant. In a country which had lived through twenty years of war and persecutions, people learned to change their skin according to circumstances, and it was not easy to track down heretics by legal methods. To carry out their persecution more effectively, the range of acceptable witnesses had to be broadened. Help from an attorney was theoretically possible, but whoever took upon himself the task of defending a heretic automatically became a suspect, so his aid had little effect. Instead of normal court procedure, the examining of witnesses behind closed doors was introduced: the reason for the Inquisition's success, as it managed to break the solidarity of even the most loyal groups.

Preceded by the gossip of a hundred tongues, a sizeable train of people would enter a city: men with pens — notaries, secretaries, scribes; and men with iron — soldiers, servants, prison guards, gathered round an inquisitor. The newcomers established themselves in the bishop's palace or a monastery, and would proclaim a 'time of mercy', usually lasting one day. Those who reported of their own free will could not be punished with death, prison or loss of property. But in return they had to provide information, from which the net of suspicion began to be woven.

People coming to the inquisitors at this stage usually accused themselves of petty or imaginary crimes, like the miller of Belcaire, who confessed that he had doubted the help of St Martin during the construction of his mill. But such a babbler, in a sweat-drenched shirt, would usually know much more, and for example could tell who had saluted one of the perfected in the street twenty years ago. The names of the informers were kept secret; two anonymous testimonies sufficed to begin an investigation. An inquisitor combined powers usually separated in a normal trial: he was investigating magistrate, prosecutor and judge. Even other representatives of the clergy participating in trials had no voice. The conscience of one person decided as to guilt or innocence.

The suspect received a summons to appear in front of the inquisatorial tribunal. During the examination he did not know his indictment, which was of great advantage to the tribunal: the accused often confessed more than was expected. After cross-examination, he was placed in prison or released under 'guarded freedom'. Prisons — a type of architecture that developed enormously at this period — were grim, as we can see in the gaols of Carcassonne and Toulouse: dark, abysmal pits in which one could neither lie nor stand upright. Hunger, thirst and irons broke even the strongest.

If the suspect proved to be unexpectedly tough, torture was used. This form of obtaining testimonies was practised in lay jurisdiction in connection with serious crimes. It was rather avoided by canonical courts. As a principle it was assumed that torture should cause neither permanent injury or bloodshed. The system of flogging had long been in use, and it was practised with skill and knowledge of human pain — there were respected experts in this field. Pope

Innocent IV's bull of 15 May 1252 finally legalized torture.

The defendant's confession was a formality, since the testimony of two informers was sufficient ground for sentencing. Informers had by no means an easy life. The denunciator of seven of the perfected was slaughtered in his own bed, and for a similar deed, a sergeant Doumenage was hanged from a dead branch. Informers preferred to give names of the dead, or of those who could hide in inaccessible castles, like Montségur or Queribus.

Admittedly the stake was saved only for the perfected, or for stubborn adherents of the Cathar Church. The rest received canonical sentences, which had a serious impact on their lives. Carrying the cross, assigned to those who made their confessions spontaneously, resulted in the boycott of the converts in societies where heresy was dominant, and bred accusations of spying for the Inquisition. Pilgrimage to remote localities was used as a penance which was a severe financial burden for the entire family; it could last from a couple of months to five years, as was the case with knights sent to the Holy Land or to Constantinople. Such punishment could befall a person who exchanged a few words with a heretic during a sea journey, or like an eleven-year-old, greeted at his parents' behest one of the perfected in the street.

Whoever thinks that the protocols of the Inquisition contain shocking material, suitable for literary treatment, is mistaken. The dialogues — as we discover by reading the *Collection Doat* — do not reveal violent responses, passion, threats, resistance and breakdowns, but a terrible monotony. The real terror is to be found in the inventories of torture chambers.

What can be found in the protocols? Names, dates, places and little else. 'During *consolamentum* administered to Auger Isorn in Fanjeaux were present: Bec from Fanjeaux, Guillaume from La Ilhe, Gaillard from Feste, Arnaud from Ovo, Jourdain from Roquefort . . .'; 'Atho Arnaud from Castelverdun demanded *consolamentum* in the house of his relatives named Covar, from Mongradail . . .'; 'Deacons Bernard Coldefi and Arnaud Guiraud lived permanently in Montréal, and their meetings were attended by Raymond from Sanchos, Peteria, wife of a Moor from Montréal . . .', and so on, page after page.

Bernard Gui, an inquisitor from the next century, is the author of an instructive work: *Libellis de ordine praedicatorum*, a textbook for inquisitors, which gives us some idea of the nature of interrogations.

'. . . The suspect is asked whether he saw or met one or many heretics; where it was, how many times, and when . . .

'*item*: whether he had any relations with them; where, when and who recommended him;

'*item*: whether he received in his dwelling one or many heretics, who in particular, and who brought them; how long they stayed with him, where they went, who visited them, whether he heard their preaching, and what it concerned;

'*item*: whether he revered heretics, or knew of anyone else revering them;

'*item*: whether he ate blessed bread with them, and how this bread was blessed . . .

'*item*: whether he saluted heretics, or saw other people saluting them . . .

'*item*: whether he believed that a person adhering to the heretic creed can be saved . . .'

Other questions concerned the views and the past of people with whom the suspect had any contact.

This means of inquiry is only apparently narrow, dull and aimless. In fact its cool, impersonal logic allowed the examiner to pursue his goal without engaging in a psychological game, trying to penetrate motives and circumstances; it paralysed the suspect with the fear we always experience when instead of a living person, we encounter stern necessity. The two orders — the moral and psychological, and that of facts — cannot be totally separated.

The poetry of the troubadours came under violent attack, as though it were not enough that courts and patrons should be in the hands of northern soldiers. 'The world has changed so much that it is impossible to recognize it,' complains Bertran d'Alamanon. Bishops and Dominicans call for the rejection of 'songs full of vanity', and the papal legate receives oaths from knights never to write verse. Lyrical poetry — a phenomenon known from other historical epochs — is replaced by weighty ideological diatribes, composed by pious rhymsters. One of the poems preserved is simply a repetition of the catechism, and would not be counted among works of literature were it not for the fact that each article of the creed is followed by this refrain:

If you do not believe, turn your eyes to the flames which

burn your companions.
Answer in one or two words only —
You will either burn in this fire, or join us.

Provençal poetry is permeated with the idea of 'sinful love', which is expounded in boring poems. *Breviári d'Amor* by Master Matfré Ermengau has 30,000 verses. Academicism enters poetry; the poem also contains a chapter on 'On the Abjectness of Flesh'. 'Satan, wanting to cause suffering to a man, ingrained him with idolatrous love for a woman. Instead of worshipping his Creator with the all his heart and the whole of his mind, he gives to a woman what belongs to God . . . Remember, whosoever reveres a woman reveres Satan, and makes the lawless demon his God.'

Of course genuine troubadours still existed, and perhaps even had clandestine meetings. The last of them, Guiraut Riquier, died in 1280, almost forty years after the stakes of Montségur. His voice is sad, the voice of a grasshopper among ruins. He was faithful to the tradition and for twenty years platonically loved the wife of the Viscount of Narbonne; in the delicacy of his sentiments, he stands among the finest representatives of the genre. Towards the end of his life, he yielded to the new current and wrote only Marian hymns, where the confusion of earthly and celestial love is almost disturbing. 'Until recently I sang of love, but truly I did not know what it was, vanity and madness taken for emotion; but now true love overwhelms me, forced to give my heart to a lady whom I shall never be able to worship as she deserves . . . I am not at all envious of others who desire her heart, and I pray for her adorers, that she will hear the supplication of each.'

The phenomenon of formalism can be studied in the troubadours' decadent poetry, as in an anatomical sample. Formalism is not the excess of metaphor or linguistic ornament, but a procedure by which old means of expression try to render a new, changed emotional and historical atmosphere. It would be naïve to claim that all troubadour poetry is a reflection of crystal purity and platonic love. History preserves the names of a number of poets like Sordel and Bertran d'Alamanon, who were libertines, notorious for their free-thinking poems and numerous scandals.

The poetry of the troubadours was always a mixture of flame and blue, but perhaps it is not the worst poetic alloy. The whole of Canto XXVI of the *Divine Comedy* is coloured by deep purple and a cold glare. In Purgatory the soul of a good poet, Arnaut Daniel, awaits the day of its liberation. Dante constructs a beautiful monument to his master. The song ends in Provençal, and has the charm of fading beauty.

But let us return to our story. It is after the Treaty of Meaux and the council in Toulouse, which has extended the Inquisition's control over the whole country. Not entirely, since irredentism still smoulders in inaccessible castles. Other countries, and especially Lombardy — with which the heretics of Toulouse and Provence had always been in close contact — were relatively peaceful, and aided their sister church.

What was to be done? The apostolic activities of the Cathars were branded with all the miseries of conspiracy. Since the cities were 'unsafe', the perfected met with believers in the mountains, in forest clearings; trailed by spies, delivered to the Inquisition yet undaunted, sneaking out at night under friendly glances, searching glances, indifferent glances of fear. Sometimes they managed to pause for a while as shoemakers, or bakers, or as doctors — a profession beloved of Cathars and suited to their charitable outlook.

In the meantime Raymond VII, following a policy of appeasement towards the Pope, made no secret of his desire to get rid of the inquisitors. Trying to prove his loyalty, he initiated the capture and burning of a number of Albigensians, among them Deacon Jehan Cambitor and his three companions hiding in Montségur. The activities of the Inquisition in the duchy were suspended for three years between 1237 and 1241. It seemed that internal peace was near.

But quite unexpectedly in 1240 an avenger appears, descending upon the country with the speed of a rising mountain stream: Raymond Trencavel, the son of the Viscount of Béziers who had died in prison. With him are the lords of occupied castles, disinherited by the French, and the exquisite Aragonese cavalry. The army advances rapidly, taking unresisting castles. But instead of striking at Carcassonne, the young leader contents himself with minor victories. The French governor organizes the defence, sends a messenger to Paris and demands aid from the Count of Toulouse, who, however, refuses in unequivocal terms. Young Trencavel furiously assaults the capital: the walls shake and crumble, but the relief led by Jean de Beaumont, Louis IX's chamberlain, forces the young warrior to retreat. The second fatal error of the campaign consists in Trencavel's marching westward, directly into the enemy's embrace, instead of retreating inland, where mountains and allies could secure a lasting defence. No wonder he has to barricade himself in Montréal. His defence, however, is so valiant that he receives honourable terms of surrender: permission to retreat with his armies and supplies to Catalonia. The French begin to recapture the lost castles, less by means of siege-machines than by negotiations, although cruelty and violence are not totally absent.

The behaviour of Raymond VII is full of contradictions. On the one hand it is known that he supported Trencavel, but on the other he promised the Pope to destroy Montségur, the capital of the Cathars. Had the Count of Toulouse joined the battle against the French, he could have changed the course of events, but he looked fatalistically upon the defeat of his ally, just like his father apathetically watching the defeat of Raymond-Roger. *Historia magister vitae?* If anyone ever tries to write a psychoanalytic account of historical figures, these events deserve their own chapter.

As if feeling that he has slept through a perfect opportunity, the Count of Toulouse throws himself into a whirlpool of artful intrigue, which results in a strong anti-French coalition including Castile, Navarre, Aragon, and even Henry III of England. Certain of the strength of his alliances, Raymond VII denounces the Treaty of Meaux. The massacre in Avignonet speeds up events.

We have said that Raymond VII obtained from Pope Gregory IX the suspension of the inquisitorial activities of the preaching brothers. But in April 1242 the Bishop of Rome dies, and the Dominicans resume their work. In December of the same year a great stake burns in Lavaur.

In May 1242 the inquisitors Guillaume Arnaud and Etienne de St Thibery arrive at the small town of Avignonet, situated in the centre of the Lauraguais province. The whole party consists of eleven members of the tribunal; among them an ex-troubadour Raymond Scriptor, archdeacon of Villelongue; the inquisitorial notary; servants. They establish their quarters in the castle of Raymond d'Alfaro. No one among the party suspects that, despite their welcome, they are already trapped. Though it is difficult to feel sympathy for an institution called the Inquisition, one has to respect the courage of people who enter unarmed a place known as a hot-bed of heresy, *de facto* in a state of war. Raymond d'Alfaro notifies the garrison of Montségur and soon sixty armed men rush to Avignonet. The rebels stop at the town gate, near the house of the lepers, where the castellan's messenger hands them twelve axes. Then, led by

Raymond himself, the sombre procession marches toward the chamber in which the inquisitors sleep. When the door breaks under the blows of axes, the friars kneel on the floor, and begin to sing the *Te Deum*. The slaughter is furious and cruel. Sources tell us that the broken skull of Guillaume Arnaud was wanted in Montségur as a drinking cup.

The temporary successes of the Count of Toulouse end when the French army sets out and speedily eliminates all his allies, including Henry III, who retreats to Bordeaux after his defeat at Taillebourg. Deserted by his vassals and allies, the Count of Toulouse remains alone, having no choice but to surrender once more to the Church and the King of France. In January 1243 a final treaty is signed in Lorris. Six years later Raymond dies without a male heir. According to the treaty, his daughter marries Alphonse de Poitiers, the brother of Louis IX. In this way Languedoc is eternally bound to the French crown.

The victors turn their eyes to the south, toward two unconquered castles, the last bastions of the Albigensians.

Montségur, the holy city of the Cathars — now only a name denoting emptiness — stands amidst a wild, mountainous landscape. The mountain and the ruins today look like one gigantic ant-hill. From the south, an almost vertical cliff of solid rock falls into the valley. The position of Montségur is mysterious, since the castle does not 'reign' over anything and guards no passage, as if its builders had other than practical reasons in mind. The very shape of the ruins resembles a long sarcophagus rather than a fortress. Wonders multiply when we follow a winding path toward the remains. The walls are bare and lack strategic characteristics: embrasures, battlements, towers. Moreover, this mysterious construction covers only a part of the mountain top. But the most amazing sight is two wide unfortified gates, unprecedented in medieval defensive architecture.

To all these puzzling details let us add an observation, that the plan of Montségur is quite exceptional. Research into the symbolism of art is not limited these days to the study of capitals, tympana and other ornamental details, so that a pentagon of bare walls can convey its hidden sense. The metaphysics of architecture are expressed also in the module, the proportion of solids, pattern of windows, orientation of the building, and even in the material and mortar. As to the castle in Montségur, its ground-plan designates the position of the rising sun at different times of the year. Hence the daring hypothesis that Montségur was not a fortress but a Cathar temple, perhaps a deposit of Manichaean culture.

Let us return to the facts. It is May 1243. Hugues d'Arcis — the new royal seneschal of Carcassonne — with his ten-thousand-strong army, sets his tents around Montségur, proclaimed a 'synagogue of Satan'. Behind a wooden palisade there are many deacons, prominent Albigensians and the perfected, with Bertrand Marty as their leader. The castle's garrison consists of fifteen knights and a hundred sergeants: no more than one hundred and fifty armed men. The French army surrounds Montségur in a semi-circle, only the southern part of the mountain is free from the siege: the almost vertical cliff plunging into an abyss, in which the defendants can see their fate.

Beginning their siege in May, the attackers thought that the sun would dry the cisterns by summer. After six months, with the situation unchanged, no one counted on heavenly assistance. Food supplies in the fortress were sufficient, and contacts with the outside world were maintained, thanks to experienced mountaineers who lowered themselves on ropes from the vertical cliff at night. Considerable differences of altitude prevented the use of siege-machines; everything seemed to indicate that the nest of Cathars could not be taken by force but only by cunning.

The defenders and inhabitants of Montségur could not expect the mighty French army to strike its tents and depart. So almost five hundred people shut in the fortress, whom a common fate had made one family, have been preparing for death for many months.

The French manage to bribe some Basque volunteers, experienced mountaineers, who with great effort manage to reach a narrow platform eighty metres from the castle. In November the royal army receives considerable reinforcements. Durand, Bishop of Albi, comes to the camp. He offers technical rather than spiritual help, being an expert constructor of siege-machines, which soon take their part in the battle. The situation is not yet hopeless, since Bertrand de la Baccalaria, a military engineer, arrives at the fortress by night. Now the defenders can reply with their own stone-throwing machines.

Winter is very hard for the besieged, there are many casualties, and rare reinforcements do not replace all those lost in fighting. Crowded into a small space of several hundred square metres, people become exhausted by the prolonged struggle. The commander of the garrison frequently sends messages to the Count of Toulouse asking whether everything is going well. The answer is affirmative, yet it is not known what this question refers to — preparations for a new uprising, a relief expedition, or negotiations.

The most dangerous weapon — stategem — is brought in. During one of the long winter nights a group of volunteers, led by a Basque guide knowing all the secret passages, crosses a dangerous crest and, deceiving the garrison with friendly shouts, massacres the defenders of the eastern tower. The passage is so dangerous that the next day the French have to admit that they would never have dared it in daylight. The situation of the defenders becomes increasingly serious, especially since Bishop Durand constructs a new machine near the walls of Montségur, which constantly pitches eighty-pound stones. The commander of defence, Pierre Roger de Mirepoix, orders the safe-keeping of treasures belonging to the Cathar Church. Two Albigensians, Mathieu and Pierre Bonnet, gather gold, silver, *pecuniam infinitam*, and hide it in a secure place.

Despite the hopelessnes of the situation for those enclosed in the fortress, the siege continues and the defenders resist. The chronicler of the crusades, Guillaume de Puylaurent, writes: 'The besieged did not know a moment of rest either at night or during the day'. The commander tries to secure help from outside. Corbario, the leader of the twenty-five Aragonese dare-devils who would constitute a select commando unit in a modern army, promises to penetrate the lines of encirclement, recapture the eastern tower and destroy the French siege-machines. The circle of the besieging army is so tight, however, that the Aragonese have to abandon their mission. The commander decides to make a desperate excursion at night. The enemies fight at the edge of an abyss in which many find their death. In the morning the battle shifts to the fortress walls, where the sisters and daughters of knights fight side by side with the men. The counter-attack is repulsed with much bloodshed. After a night full of the moaning of the wounded, the trampled, and those fallen into the abyss from the walls of Montségur, a horn can be heard. Raymond de Pereille and Pierre Roger de Mirepoix go to the enemy's camp to negotiate. Montségur surrenders after nine months of siege.

The victors were so exhausted that they accepted the majority of the proposed conditions, which in effect proved to be quite advantageous. The defenders could keep Montségur for fifteen days, in order to celebrate an Albigensian holiday in mid–March. They were forgiven their past misdeeds, even the slaughter in Avignonet. The soldiers could leave the fortress with their weapons and belongings. They would be examined by the Inquisition, but only light punishments were to be exacted. Other persons sheltering in the castle could go free if they renounced heresy, otherwise they were to go to the stake. The fortress was to be handed over to the King of France.

So, after the signing of the treaty on 2 March 1244, the longed for peace reigned in the town; fifteen days of mercy before death, fifteen days of farewell between those who would descend into the valleys with the spring winds, and those who would be consumed by the flames above. It is highly admirable that, during the armistice, six women and eleven men converted to Catharism, which amounted to choosing a martyr's death. Martyrs of destroyed religions are not canonized.

On 16 March 1244, French soldiers, bishops and inquisitors entered Montségur. Raymond de Pereille, one of the defence commanders, parted forever with his wife and his youngest daughter who chose the stake. It was not the only farewell of families torn apart.

Soldiers built a huge stake at the foot of a mountain, in a place now called 'Cramatchs' — from *prat dels crematz*, the field of those who were burned. Dry wood at that time of year is scarce, so instead of the usual construction of twigs and poles to which the condemned were tied, they built a palisade strewn with a thick layer of brushwood. They pushed the chained Albigensians into this horrible enclosure. The palisade was set alight from all sides. The wounded and the sick were thrown inside. The heat was so intense that witnesses had to retreat from the pyre. The singing of the clergy and the moaning of the dying merged.

At night, when human bodies still smouldered, three Albigensians hiding in the cellars of Montségur sneaked out and lowered themselves down the vertical cliff. They carried away the remaining treasure, the holy books, and their testimony to martyrdom.

Heavy, nauseating smoke descends into the valleys and spreads across history.

DEFENCE OF THE TEMPLARS

H<small>IGH JURY</small>,

The role of the defence in this trial, lasting six and a half centuries, is not an easy one. We cannot summon the prosecutors, witnesses or defendants, whose bodies were consumed by fire, their ashes scattered by the wind. Apparently everything speaks against them. The prosecutor has thrown down upon the table a pile of documents, from which an unbiased reader can reconstruct a sombre picture of the crimes and misdeeds of the accused, and find convincing proof of guilt. Convincing, since the accused level the most severe accusations at themselves. We shall make it our task to call the reliability of these documents into question and to encourage you, High Jury, to read between the lines, to make you understand the background and mechanism, as well as the methods of the investigation. Thus we must return to events preceding this cool evening when the stake was set alight. The leaders of the Templars, Jacques de Molay and Geoffroi de Charney, died in its flames. The time and place of the execution: 18 March 1314, a small island on the Seine within the borders of Paris. The sole mercy granted to the executed was to die facing the white towers of Notre-Dame. The last words: 'The bodies belong to the King of France, but the souls belong to God.'

Experts usually treat these final words with scepticism. Historians question their authenticity. But their value consists in the fact that they are the creation of collective consciousness, an attempt at synthesis, a definition of fate. Please accept them, High Jury, as yet another uncertain testimony.

And now, let us try to reconstruct briefly the history of the Templar Order.

Among the crusaders setting off to the Holy Land in 1095, there was an elderly nobleman from Champagne. As we know, this expedition resulted in the conquest of Jerusalem in 1099 and the creation of the Kingdom. But only a small number of western knights remained in Palestine. The vast majority, exhausted by bickering and the toils of war, returned home. The fate of the young Kingdom of Jerusalem, surrounded by a sea of infidels, was far from secure. In order to keep this island, not only stronger walls were needed, but also a new society. The old method of Greek and Roman colonists had its advocate in the chaplain of Baldwin I, Foucher de Chartres. 'We, who were people of the West,' he wrote, 'have become people of the East. We, who were dwellers in Reims or Chartres, became citizens of Tyre and Antioch; we have already forgotten the place of our birth, and many do not know it at all. Some of us have houses and servants in this country, which we will give to our descendants as their heritage. Others have married women who are not their countrywomen, but are the natives of Syria, Armenia or are even Saracens, who have received the grace of baptism. Some tend to their vineyards, others to their fields; they still speak in different tongues, but they already begin to understand each other; those who were poor in their country, God made rich; those who did not even have a manor, now rule over cities. Why should they return to the West, if they do so well in the East?' It is a noteworthy text, even if we reject the element of obvious official propaganda.

The new monarchy was more democratic, so to speak, and more republican than many monarchies in the West. Royal authority was limited by a parliament of both barons and burghers. And its voice was decisive in important matters, such as taxes. The peasants were free. Religious freedom was respected. In many temples there was the practice of *simultaneum* — religious celebration according to various rites and creeds. The Torah, Koran and the Bible, on which one swore oaths in front of tribunals, co-existed peacefully — probably for the first time in history, and not only in courtrooms. Of course the real picture changed according to events, social tensions, and was far from ideal. However, one should be aware of this effort to create a multi-racial, multi-religious society.

Let us return now to our knight from Champagne. His name was Hugues de Payns, and he was, as was said, of advanced age but brave and vigorous. He has exchanged the green hills of his native country for the parched land of Palestine, but not for the material profit advertised so convincingly by Chaplain Foucher. With a handful of companions he has founded an order whose task is to defend pilgrims from bandits and Saracens, and to protect wells. It is, in short, a kind of roadside militia. King Baldwin gave them a dwelling situated on the site of the Temple of Solomon, hence their name: the Templars. They took vows of purity and poverty. An ancient seal provides evidence, depicting two knights riding on one horse. If we can anticipate future events, High Jury, this second knight was interpreted during the investigation as Satan, the evil instigator. The inventiveness and imagination of slanderers, High Jury, knows no bounds. Hugues de Payns travels to France and England where the new Order is enthusiastically received in both lay and clerical circles. There is a flow of benefices and donations. The Order is joined by princes and barons. The ecumenical council in Troyes establishes its rule in 1128, and the highest moral authority in Europe, St Bernard, becomes its spiritual sponsor. In his well-known *Liber Ad Milites Templi De Laude Novae Militiae*, he contrasts the austere, virtuous knights of the Temple with the newly enriched, vain knights of the West.

'They dislike all excess in food and clothing, and they strive only for what is necessary. They live together, without women and children . . . offensive words, superfluous acts, unmitigated laughter, complaining and grumbling if noticed, do not pass among them unpunished. They abhor chess and dice, they are repulsed by hunting. They find no pleasure in the mindless chase of fowl; they are revolted by and avoid mimes, magicians, jugglers, light songs and jokes. They cut their hair short, and they know from the Apostles that care for hair humiliates a man. No one ever saw them use a comb; they wash rarely, their beards are rough, full of dust, stained by heat and toil.'

In Jerusalem the Templars soon took over two mosques, under which there were huge vaults designed as stables. In fact the fortified Templum was a city within a city. Life was isolated, austere and simple. Meals were served in a vast refectory with unadorned walls. The knights ate in silence and left a portion of their food for the poor. When one of the brothers died, his ration was given to a beggar for fourteen days. Three days a week no meat was served, twice a year there was a total fast. The day began with a mass celebrated two hours before sunrise. Then each knight visited the stables, groomed his horse and inspected his weapons. At sunrise there was another mass, and during the day there were scores of obligatory prayers. Lunch, then roll-call supervised by the Master. Vespers, prayers, and silence until the end of the day. The rule also contained a penal code. Ten offences were punishable with exclusion from the Order, or even life imprisonment. These were: simony to gain admittance to the Order, repetition of conversations heard in the chapter, stealth, desertion from the battlefield, robbery, murder of a Christian, sodomy, heresy, (this offence, High Jury, should be kept in mind), lying and abandoning the Order.

Laudatory remarks by St Bernard of Clairvaux (o paradox of history) made the Templars powerful bankers in the Middle Ages. During the Second Crusade, the Order had properties throughout Europe. Pilgrims travelling to the Holy Land, in order to avoid risk, would deposit money in one of their houses and receive the equivalent in Jerusalem. That they soon became lenders not only to the King of Jerusalem, but also to sovereigns of England and France is evidence of their financial power. This very fact, High Jury, as we shall try to demonstrate, became the source of their downfall. The Order's profits did not enrich its members. There was a strict rule that if a dying brother was found carrying money, he had to be buried in unconsecrated ground.

The Templars, who from a handful of monk-knights became an army of many thousands, were known as outstanding warriors. Let us call on the evidence of Louis VII, who wrote to Abbot Suger: 'I cannot imagine how we would be able to hold our ground in this country (the Holy Land) without their assistance and presence. We ask you, therefore, that you double your kindness to them, so that they feel our intercession.' There is reference further on to the large sum of two thousand marks lent to the sovereign, and a request that the regent-abbot return it to the Order in France. Until the middle of the twelfth century we cannot find a single document mentioning the Templars which does not extol their knightly virtues and loyalty.

And then? It is obvious, High Jury, that every social organism has its bright and dark moments. But the prosecutor has omitted all those facts which could speak for the defendants. He has ignored the heroic period of the Order, underscoring only those moments which show its decadence and secularization, abandonment of its ideals, its vanity and intrigues. The defence is far from a blind glorification of the Templars: we shall not challenge the prosecution where documents and sources testify against the Order. We propose, however, that these facts should not be treated in isolation, but be judged against the political and social background of their time.

The history of the Kingdom of Jerusalem belongs to one of the most complicated and obscure chapters of history. While studying this period, we have the impression of looking into a simmering cauldron of passions, intrigues, desire for fame and fortune, unnatural ambitions, complex political and dynastic machinations. The Templars, who had become a force of over ten thousand knights, could not stand aside and watch events on which not only their prestige and profit rested, as the prosecutor claims, but also their lives. They were forced to join in power-politics. But let us add, High Jury, that they also participated in every great battle, sharing the crusaders' miseries for two centuries: imprisonment, long sieges, marches through the desert, wounds and death. The crusaders came and went, and the miscalculations of their military raids fell on the heads of those who, like the Templars, decided to hold on to the patch of conquered land until the very end. This is, High Jury, indispensable to our understanding of the affairs and politics of the Order.

In 1187 Saladin recaptures Jerusalem from the crusaders. For a long time the Kingdom is without a capital. Two years later the Third Crusade begins. Three great sovereigns could have changed the run of bad luck, yet it happened otherwise. Frederick Barbarossa was eliminated by an accident — death in the undertow of a river. Richard the Lion-Heart from the outset rivalled Philip Augustus. Upon learning that the French monarch paid his followers three pieces of gold, Richard sold Cyprus to the Templars and announced that those who chose his banner would receive four gold pieces. As a result, Philip withdrew from the expedition. What is more, despite Saladin's intervention, in which the Order served as an intermediary (later this fact will be used to prove that the Templars had good relations, or even plotted, with the Muslims), he murdered 2,700 captives, which provoked the massacre of French prisoners in retaliation. Nevertheless, the Templars were the vanguard of the ill-fated expedition, from which Richard withdrew upon learning that John Lackland had claimed his throne. He left Palestine on a Templar ship, dressed in a cassock of the Order.

In the second decade of the thirteenth century, the already bad situation of the Kingdom of Jerusalem was worsened by the Mongol invasion. Pope Honorius III persuaded the German Emperor, Frederick II, to marry the heiress to the Jerusalem throne, Isabelle, the daughter of Jean de Brienne. The Emperor reached hungrily for the fruit presented to him, forced the King to leave and entertained an alliance with the Sultan of Egypt, which brought about his excommunication.

Let us add that the policy of the Templars was based on just the opposite premise: they tried to maintain good relations with the Sultan of Damascus, quite effectively, and relied on the old principle of exploiting differences in the opponent's camp. Through the Emperor's alliances Jerusalem was reclaimed, and Frederick illegally proclaimed himself King. The capital was at last in Christian hands, which might seem to be a signal for pride and rejoicing. But it turned out that according to a secret agreement with the Sultan, Jerusalem was not to be fortified or defended. The entire district which belonged to the Templars, who from the beginning opposed the excommunication of the ruler, was given to the Muslims. The Emperor also endowed them with property which was not his, namely the fortresses of the Order: Safet, Toron, Gaza, Darum, Krak and Montréal. As if that were not enough, Frederick took over the Order's castle, Château Pélerin.

One can hardly be surprised by the Templars' rage. They notified the Emperor that if he did not leave Palestine, 'they would lock him in a place from which he would never depart'. Frightened by the uprising of the Guelphs, Frederick set out for Europe, leaving the power and care of the Kingdom to the Teutonic Knights (well known to Poles and hostile toward the Templars). From a safe distance he initiated a campaign of slander against the Order which dared to oppose his will. He repeated the old argument discrediting the Templars in the eyes of the Christian world: they plot with the infidels. He himself, with typical cynicism, assumed Eastern habits, maintaining good relations with the Sultan of Damascus. At his court he was host to the ambassador of the Sultan of Egypt. He even received the envoys of the Ismail sect of the Assassins, who, in all probability, killed at his instigation his opponent, Duke Louis of Bavaria.

Finally in 1248 there came the crusade of Louis IX. One might expect that this time there would be harmonious cooperation between the crusaders and the local knights. The disinterestedness of the leader of the expedition and his good relations with the Templars should have assured that much. Unfortunately, the plans of the expedition were prepared in Europe, and completely overlooked local conditions. Against the advice of the Templars, the hopeless campaign against Egypt recommenced. Despite the Order's opposition, its knights formed the vanguard of the army lead by the King's brother, Robert, Count of Artois. The Nile split the army into two parts. Against the arguments of the Templars, Robert decided not to wait for the rest of the forces, and after a short, victorious battle with the Turks, moved into the territory. Yet in the narrow streets of Mansourah the crusaders were met by the Sultan Baybars and his Mamelukes. From the roofs and barricades came a rain of missiles. Trapped, lacerated with arrows like hedgehogs, the crusaders were smashed to pieces. The Sultan's counter-attacks resulted in a disastrous situation for the royal army: scurvy, hunger, and ditches filled with corpses, forced Louis to surrender. There came captivity, from which the invalid King had to be ransomed for the staggering sum of £500,000.

Aware of the political misjudgements, in which they had no part, the Templars started negotiations with Damascus. Learning of this, Louis IX took strict disciplinary measures, including the dismissal of the Grand Master of the Order and the exile of those who tried to make a treaty without his consent.

High Jury, these three selected episodes illustrate the permanently endangered state of the Order, growing misunderstandings, numerous humiliations — the web of intrigues in which it was snared.

The sole consolation was the favour of the popes, who interceded effectively in a number of conflicts. In the end, even this support was lost.

The Marshal of the Templars, Etienne de Sissey, was summoned to Rome in 1263 and stripped of his powers. If we are to believe the chronicler Gérard de Montréal, the reason was an amorous affair, a notorious and compromising rivalry for the favours of a certain beautiful lady from Acre.

The final act of the drama began on 5 April 1291 in this very town, Acre. It was a port and defended itself for two and a half months. The situation of the crusaders was hopeless. Though they could have easily abandoned the fortress, a group of monk-knights together with the Grand Master, Guillaume de Beaujeu, defended it to the end. Acre was drowned in the onslaught The Kingdom of the Crusaders ceased to exist.

High Jury, after this extensive but necessary introduction, the defence will address itself to the central issue: that is, to the trial of the Templars (then led by the Grand Master, Jacques de Molay) staged by the grandson of Louis IX, Philip the Fair, King of France. His hard rule was autocratic almost in the modern sense of the word, and he is justly considered as a prototypical European dictator. His numerous wars exhausted the country's treasury. His rule was characterized by a series of great economic crises. Almost from the day he was enthroned, Philip was in conflict with the Holy See, which, as we know, led to the Pope's captivity in Avignon. These political elements played a decisive role in the trial of the Templars.

The trial was initiated, High Jury, in order to eliminate power independent of the state. It was started — I shall not hesitate to claim — in order to appropriate the Order's wealth. It was started in order to prevent the Templars, who were the third international power, from siding with the Vatican in the confrontation between the King and the Pope. We shall attempt to demonstrate that the religious, moral and ideological accusations voiced during the trial were but a smoke-screen for the political motives of the entire operation.

Despite the loss of their properties in the Kingdom of Jerusalem, the Order was a force which every realistic sovereign had to take into account. Twenty thousand armed Templars could decide the fate of wars. They had properties and castles not only in France, but also in Italy, Sicily, Portugal, Castile, Aragon, England, Germany, Bohemia, Hungary, and even Poland, where they kept two battalions and supported King Henry the Pious in the Battle of Legnica. Two centres, however, had special importance: Cyprus — the strategic centre and base for expeditions to the East, and Paris — the political centre.

In the French capital the walled Templars' quarter was a city within a city, with separate jurisdiction, administration and the right of asylum. Philip the Fair's relations with the papacy were clear and unscrupulous. Bulls flying over 'our dear son', and the persuasive *Ausculta fili* were viewed like exotic birds from a distant epoch. The ultimatum issued by the Council of Rome in 1302 had only one effect: the King established the Estates General which accepted his politics 'in the name of the nation'. What are two theoretical swords for someone who trusts only the one in hand? The response to Boniface VIII's proposed excommunication of Philip was to send an envoy, Guillaume de Nogaret, to Italy to bring the Pope by force to France.

What was the Templars' relation to Philip? The prosecutor has told us that according to numerous proofs, retired officers (that is how one could describe the Order's situation after the fall of the Kingdom of Jerusalem) like to plot. The facts, however, testify to their deep loyalty toward the French sovereign, and at least their financial, but quite decisive, support of his actions. Nothing foreshadows the conflict, there are no warning signs, but in the inner circle of royal counsellors a plan of attack ripens. In the same year that the King declares 'our genuine and particular attachment to the Order', an occasion arises to provide the necessary pretext for the affair. As the High Jury has probably guessed, we are talking about the secret denunciation.

At the beginning of 1305, a certain Noffo Dei, a Florentine and — let us add — a criminal, gives testimony from prison, which indicted the Templars with apostasy and bad conduct. In addition, the King is feverishly collecting information from brothers expelled from the Order. The castles and homes of the Templars are invaded by an army of spies.

At the same time, unconnected to the denunciations, the new Pope, Clement V, proposes a merger of the Templar Order with the Order of the Hospitallers. The purpose was to join forces before a new crusade, which was not in fact launched. The Grand Master, Jacques de Molay, rejects this suggestion. One can guess that his motive was not just pride, but the difficulty of reconciling two rules. This move would prove tragic in its results.

When we reflect, High Jury, on the trial of the Templars, we should note that Philip the Fair was not acting solely on cold calculation. His attitude towards the Order was marked by authentic passion. It is a psychological moment not without importance. We shall try to explain.

Towards the end of 1305, after the third currency devaluation, the *petit peuple* of Paris rebelled. The upheavals reached such a state that the King with his family were forced to escape to the Templars' fortress, the famous Tour du Temple, where he endured a humiliating siege by the 'populace'. Within a few days the leaders of the rebellion were hanged at the gates of Paris, but the taste of defeat was bitter. Nothing humiliates a monarch more than the feeling of gratitude, especially towards those whom one plans to pronounce criminals. In the same year Philip conducted a dress rehearsal for the trial of the Templars. The object of the manoeuvres was a defence-less nation, the Jews, whose property was confiscated, they them-selves cruelly tortured, and finally condemned to exile.

Philip the Fair knew that in a widespread action the political police should act swiftly to eliminate any danger of resistance. The thunderbolt must strike before the victim sees the lightning.

On Thursday 12 October 1307, Jacques de Molay walked beside the King during the funeral of the wife of Charles of Valois. On Friday morning all the Templars in France were arrested. We must bow, High Jury, in sad admiration to this unprecedented display of police precision.

The prosecutor has said that the imprisonment of the Templars surprised no one, that charges against them were voiced many times. He added that Philip the Fair conferred with Pope Clement V over this matter, but again he omitted the background of these talks. It is known that these negotiations concerned a new crusade. The Pope wanted to send as its leader the dangerous kidnapper of popes, de Nogaret, hoping to break his political career and return him to a virtuous path. The idea of a crusade, however, was totally un-welcome to Philip. He presented its difficulties, claiming trouble in the Templar Order, which, as usual, was to constitute the nucleus of the army. The prosecution also has ignored the fact that the Order's Master, Jacques de Molay himself, asked the Pope for an in-vestigation to clear the Order of frequent yet vague accusations. Clement V in turn, unable to find reliable evidence against the Templars, in September 1307 asked Philip the Fair for the results of his investigation. It is obvious, High Jury, that the King could not compromise himself by providing testimonies of criminals or obviously bribed brothers who had been expelled from the Order. One had to extract, by means of a hot iron, self-accusations from those who currently belonged to the Order.

The warrant of arrest sent to barons, prelates and royal officials in the provinces is a masterpiece of rhetoric: 'It is a bitter thing, a lamentable matter, a matter truly horrible to contemplate, and terrible to hear about — an odious crime, an execrable evil, an appalling act, a detestable disgrace — truly inhuman deeds have reached our ears, causing our deep astonishment, and most shocked repulsion . . .'. High Jury, please count the adjectives. Abundance of adjectives is a sure sign not only of bad poetry, but also of accusations weak on fact; further on the text contains nothing but the gurgle of rage.

The investigation immediately followed the arrests and was conducted by lay authorities. Instructions for the commissioners recommend 'thorough examinations, if necessary with the use of torture'. The accused are faced with the alternative: either confess and be pardoned, or die at the stake.

Progress in our civilization, High Jury, consists mainly in the fact that simple tools for splitting heads were replaced by hatchet-words, which have the advantage of psychologically paralysing an opponent. Such words are: 'mind-debaucher', 'witch' and 'heretic'. The Templars were accused of heresy, chiefly to deprive the Pope of the possibility of intervening on their behalf. Moreover, the battle was difficult from the start. Philip the Fair had power, the Holy See just diplomacy.

Now comes the moment most taxing for the defence, and it is hardly surprising that the prosecution placed its emphasis here. It is true that Jacques de Molay admitted publicly, in the presence of representatives of the Church, theologians and the University of Paris, that there was a long-standing custom practised during the admission of new brothers: they denounced Christ and spat on the Cross. Another dignitary of the Order, Geoffroi de Charney, gave similar testimony, making the exception, however, that he himself was never involved in such practices, as contrary to the principles of the Creed. One should add that both confessions were made just twelve days after the arrests, which may suggest that they were spontaneous. Let us remember, however, that for suspects under investigation time is not measured in days, but in hours, and that conforming to royal instructions, the investigative apparatus worked 'thoroughly'.

It is quite probable that the Grand Master, who as the trial demonstrated was a very naïve politician, was promised that public confession would save the Order. Moreover, the very act of spitting on the Cross does not indicate apostasy, but according to many experts is an element of initiation, dialectical in character. One might recall the well-known ritual of knighting, when a symbolic slap in the face is the only affront that a knight must endure without return. In addition, the testimonies of various Templars are contradictory. Some say that they were spitting not on the Cross, but to the side. Others deny the practice. Geoffroi de Gonneville explained that the custom was introduced by a bad Master, who having been in Saracen captivity, regained his freedom by renouncing Christ, though the accusee could not identify this Master.

Brother Gérard de Pasagio declared: 'A novice entering the Order was presented with a wooden crucifix and asked if that was God. He answered that it was the image of the Crucified. A receiving brother told him: "Do not believe this. That is but a piece of wood. Our Lord is in Heaven".' It is evidence against idolatory, of which the Templars were accused, and a proof of the high spiritualization of their faith. In short, High Jury, the testimonies were contradictory as to the custom itself and as to its origin. More importantly, neither written records nor preserved rules contain such an ordinance.

Similarly in the case of the idol, which was supposed to be venerated by the Templars, and over which a sea of ink was spilled, so that even if it were an angel it would have turned into a devil. The Grand Inquisitor, Guillaume de Paris, instructed the investigative organs to quiz the accused about the statue with a human head and a huge beard. Again the statements are contradictory and vague. For some it was a statue of wood, for others of silver and leather; feminine or masculine; bare-faced or bearded; resembling a cat or a pig; it had one head, or two, or even three. Despite the confiscation of all sacred objects, nothing resembling the descriptions could be found.

What we have here, High Jury, is a classic case of collective psychosis. And we — who know the logic of fear, the psychopathology of a hunted man, the theory of group behaviour in the face of extermination — we should not believe it. Let us remember that the medieval imagination was haunted by the devil. Who could better explain to the tortured, to those imprisoned in dungeons, the sense of their fate?

What remains, High Jury, is the name of that demon. It has survived until our time, being the subject of numerous experts' consideration. Not the object, but the word is the sole evidence in this trial. Let us utter this word at last: Baphomet.

A German expert, the Orientalist Baron von Hammer-Purgstall, finds its origin in the word *Bahumid*, which was supposed to mean an ox. Hence the conclusion that it was a case of the cult of the Golden Calf, of which the Templars in fact were accused. This thesis did not hold water, and the author himself later changed it into an equally unconvincing one. A specialist in the history of the Templars and a prominent scholar, Emil Michelet, saw in it an acronym which according to the Cabbala should be read backwards: *TEMpli Omnium Hominum Pacis ABbas*. It was noted also that the name could originate from a port held by the Templars: Bapho, where in ancient times stood the temple of Astarte — Venus and Moon, Virgin and Mother — to whom children were sacrificed. This hypothesis was mentioned by the prosecutor, who followed a line of fantastic charges against the Templars, including cannibalism.

A rather more plausible explanation, at least from a philological point of view, was provided at the turn of the nineteenth century by an outstanding Arabist, Sylvestre de Sacy, who derived the name from the mispronounced name of Mahomet. This theory was supported by a poem composed by a Templar, Oliver, in the *langue d'oc*, '*E Bafonet obra de son poder*' ('And Mahomet has flared with his might'). It is by no means proof, as the prosecution would have it, of the infiltration of the Templars' esoteric doctrine by Islam. Though they were attracted to a certain extent to the religions of the East, no document indicates that they were a religious sect. In their minds the perspective on faith was certainly enlarged. What was an axiom for every French nobleman setting forth on a crusade — that Christianity was the only religion worthy of its name — was unsettled by new contacts and experiences. The Koran, recognizing Christ as one of the Prophets, certainly facilitated that process.

Let us return from the East, which at the time of our story is just a fading echo, to France where the life and honour of the Order is at stake. As becomes a modern leader, Philip the Fair could use propaganda with outstanding skill. As the tortured moan in the dungeons throughout France, the King writes a letter to European sovereigns denouncing the 'crimes' of the Templars. However, not all gave credence to the charges. The King of England, Edward II, saw them as calumnies and conveyed his favourable disposition towards the Templars to the kings of Portugal, Castile, Aragon and Sicily, and to the Pope. One can easily conclude that the allegedly bad reputation of the Templars was not as universal as the prosecution would have us believe.

After the initial self-accusation extracted from the Grand Master, the Templars had only one hope: that they would be entrusted to Church jurisdiction, or, more precisely, that they would be judged by the Pope. And in fact at the end of 1307, the King agreed to send the prisoners to Clement V. Hearing this news, the Templars revoked their testimonies. According to tradition, Jacques de Molay did so in front of a crowd gathered in a church, showing them the marks of his torture.

Seeing the threads of the intrigue slipping through his fingers, Philip presses the pedal of propaganda — this time internal propaganda. Letters circulate in Paris accusing the Pope of being bribed by the Templars. Nothing fosters emotion better than pecuniary arguments. Having excited the mob, the King turns towards parliament and the University of Paris for support of his anti-papal politics, demanding a statement on the Templars. The University, however, responds that matters of heresy should be judged by an ecclesiastical tribunal, offering additional proof that not all public opinion turned against the Order. The intellectuals, as usual, proved unreliable; but the parliament which assembled in May 1308 in Tours — admittedly incomplete, since many noblemen preferred to excuse their absence than to take part in the farce — after acquainting itself with the forced testimonies, declares that the Templars deserve death. Strengthened by public opinion, Philip travels to Poitiers to meet the Pope.

Clement V confronted the King in a masterly way, by immediately turning the conversation to matters of the crusade while keeping silent about the trial of the Templars. The King had no alternative but to use his faithful dignitaries of the Church, the archbishops of Narbonne and Bourges, who together with royal confidants violently attacked the Order, the indifference of ecclesiastical power and spared no offensive words against the Pope himself. Clement V maintained his position. He even remarked that some of the Templars' testimonies seemed unconvincing, and in order to gain time promised that the Council of Vienne, due to gather the next year, would address itself to the problem of the Order. He also demanded to see the principal defendants.

The defendants were transported by armed convoy from Paris to Poitiers. The journey was suddenly interrupted in Chinon, on the pretext of indisposition of the accused. Beyond any doubt, High Jury, it was a scheme prepared in advance. Chinon, whose sombre walls have been preserved to this day, was a suitable place for that interlude, with its immense dungeons. When the Pope's envoys reached the place of new torment, accompanied by the sworn enemies of the Templars, de Nogaret and de Plaisians, the accused kept silent or admitted their guilt. Returned to the dungeons, they could write their testament on the walls.

While examining the dossier of the case, it is easy to note how often the interrogated retract their testimonies, only to return, after some days, to the most severe self-accusations. One cannot explain it except by the use of fire, cauldron, estrapade, iron boots and hoop-iron. The defence takes the liberty of quoting fragments from some of the testimonies.

Ponsard de Gizy, 29 November 1309:
'Asked if he was subjected to torture, he answered that in the three months which elapsed before the confession made by him in the presence of the Lord Bishop of Paris, he was thrown into a pit with his hands tied so tightly that blood ran to his nails; he had said then that if they tormented him, he would recant previous testimonies and say everything they wanted. He was ready for anything, only to make his suffering short: a beheading, the stake, submersion in boiling water for the honour of the Order, but could not bear the long torment he had to endure in prison for over two years.'

Brother Bernard from Albi:
'I was tortured so much, so long was I interrogated and kept in the fire, that my feet were burned, and I felt my bones breaking inside me.'

Brother Aimery de Villiers-le-Duc, 13 May 1310:
'The protocol says that the accused was pale and terrified. He had sworn with his hand on the altar that the crimes of which the Order was accused were an invention. "If I lie, let my body and soul be consumed by Hell right here in this place." When his previous testimonies were read to him, he answered: "Yes, I confessed many misdeeds, but that was because of the torment inflicted upon me by royal knights, Guillaume de Marcilly and Hugues de la Celle during interrogation. Yesterday I saw fifty-four of my brothers taken on carts to be burned alive . . . Ah, if I am going to die at the stake, I shall confess that I am very afraid of death, that I cannot endure it, I shall yield to terror . . . I shall confess under oath, in front of you, in front of any one, to any crime you charge the Order with; I shall admit I have killed the Lord if they so demand." '

I would like to stress, High Jury, the psychological side of death at the stake. The animal fear of fire rests on the knowledge that it will inflict the most acute pain. What spiritual strength is needed to keep faith, in order to carry at least the smallest part of ourselves through this destructive element. For medieval society the taste of ash was not, as for us, the taste of nothingness. Death at the stake was the vestibule of Hell, a never-ending stake where bodies suffer inextinguishable pain. The physical fire merged with the spiritual. Present suffering foreshadows eternal torment. Heaven — the domain of the chosen, the cool, silent masses of air — was in the eyes of the dying remote and inaccessible.

At the beginning of 1309, the investigation is renewed. This new phase is characterized by tightening of the screws of the machine for extracting testimonies (in Paris alone, thirty-six Templars died during interrogation). On the other hand, a seemingly inexplicable thing happens: the unprecedented resistance of the prisoners, who abandon all tricks and politics. Jacques de Molay states that he will defend the Order, but only in front of the Pope. Other brothers make similar declarations. By 2 May the number of Templars ready to defend the Order has grown to five hundred and sixty-three. The answer to this mass resistance is a stake at which fifty-four Templars perish. The old Roman method of decimation triumphs.

In June 1311 the investigation is closed and the dossier sent to the Pope. The Council of Vienne did not bring the expected relief for the Order. These were the years of the Avignon captivity, and the Pope considered the case as lost. The Bull *Vox in excelso* of 22 March 1312 dissolved the Order, yet it did not contain a condemnation of the Templars. By the Bull *Ad providam* of 2 May, their property was to be handed over to the Hospitallers. The blood of the brothers of the Temple did not turn into Philip's gold. The prisons of France, however, were full; and something had to be done with the dignitaries of the Order, who wanted to defend themselves, 'since we do not even have four pennies to pay for a fresh defence'. They constantly demand to be brought before a papal tribunal.

The investigation, however, was over and the envoys of Clement V assisted passively at the passing of the sentence. The leaders of the Templars faced life imprisonment. The sentence of Jacques de Molay and Geoffroi de Charney was read in Notre-Dame Cathedral. A great crowd listened in silence; but before the reading of the sentence could be completed, both men — perhaps the dignified

Gothic of Notre-Dame exercised its influence — faced the people and shouted down the charges of crime and heresy levelled against the Templars whose rule 'was always sacred, right and Catholic'. A sentry's heavy hand fell on the mouth of the Master to muffle the last words of the condemned. The cardinals handed over the recalcitrant to the court of Paris. Philip the Fair commanded burning at the stake on the same day. To appease his anger, he gave to the flames another thirty-six unrepentant brothers.

High Jury, that appears to be the end of the drama of the Templar Order. Experts rummage the tombs for a clue to the mystery. Sometimes they come across the gifts of eternity, sometimes they are fascinated by the smile of the alleged Baphomet found on a portal. The defence set forth a more modest task: examination of the tools.

In history nothing remains closed. The methods used against the Templars enriched the repertoire of power. That is why we cannot leave this distant affair under the pale fingers of archivists.

PIERO DELLA FRANCESCA

For Jarosław Iwaszkiewicz

FRIENDS say: well, you've been there and seen a lot; you liked Duccio, the Dorian columns, the stained glass at Chartres and the Lascaux bulls — but tell us what you've chosen for yourself, who is the painter closest to your heart, the one you'd never exchange. A reasonable question since every love, if true, should efface the previous one, should enter, overwhelm and demand exclusiveness. So I pause and reply: Piero della Francesca.

The first meeting: in London at the National Gallery. A cloudy day. A choking fog descends upon the city. Though I did not intend to visit sights, I was forced to find shelter against the stifling damp. The sensation came unexpectedly. From the first room it was apparent: the collection surpasses the Louvre. Never had I seen so many masterpieces at once. Perhaps this is not the best way to become acquainted with art. A concert programme should contain, apart from Scarlatti, Bach, Mozart, a Noskowski — for instruction rather than out of perversity.

I stayed longest with a painter whose name I had only known from books. The painting was *The Nativity*, an unusual composition full of light and serious joy. The sensation was similar to my first encounter with Van Eyck. It is difficult to define such an aesthetic shock. The picture roots you to one spot. You cannot step back or move closer or (as with modern painting) smell the paint and examine the facture treatment.

The background of *The Nativity* is a humble shed, or rather a crumbling brick wall with a light, slanted roof. The Christ-child rests on a patch of grass worn like an old rug. Behind the child stands a choir of five angels, strong as columns, who face the spectator with their bare feet and earthly appearance. Their peasant faces contrast with the luminous countenance of the Madonna (as in Baldovinetti) who kneels to the right in silent adoration. The fragile candles of her beautiful arms are alight. Beyond we see the massive torso of a bull, a donkey, two 'Flemish' shepherds and St Joseph turning his profile to the viewer. At the sides are two landscapes like windows through which sparkling light pours. Despite some damage, the colours are as clear and resonant as stained glass. Painted in the last years of the artist's career, it is 'Piero's evening prayer to childhood and dawn'.

On the opposite wall *The Baptism of Christ*. One of the first surviving canvases of Piero. It has the same solemn architectural serenity as *The Nativity*, though painted earlier. The solid flesh of the figures contrasts with the light, harmonious landscape. There is a finality in the leaves cast like cards upon the sky — a moment becomes eternity.

Goethe's wise dictum: '*Wer den Dichter will verstehen, muss in Dichters Lande gehen.*' As the fruits of light, paintings should be viewed under the artist's native sun. Sassetta seems out of place even in the most attractive American museums. Hence the pilgrimage to Piero della Francesca. Since my means were modest, I surrendered to chance and adventure. The story does not follow a chronology so relished by historians.

Perugia. This sombre town dwells in the green-golden Umbrian landscape. A most dismal town, imprisoned in dark marble. Hung on a high rock above the Tiber, it has been compared to a giant's hand — changing during its cruel and violent history into an Etruscan, Roman and Gothic town. It is symbolized by the Palazzo dei Priori, a powerful edifice with metal ornaments and a wall bent like molten iron. A fantastic labyrinth of streets, stairs, passages and dungeons — an architectural replica of the inhabitants' anxious spirit — lies behind the square which was once the site of the ruined Palazzo Baglioni, but is now occupied by elegant hotels.

'*I Perugini sono angeli o demoni,*' said Aretino. The town's coat of arms: a griffin with bared mouth and tenacious talons. At the height of its power, the Perugian Republic ruled over Umbria defended by one hundred and twenty castles. The temperament of its citizens was best exemplified by the Baglioni family whose members seldom died a natural death. They were vengeful and cruel, though refined enough to slaughter their enemies on beautiful summer evenings. The first 'pictures' of the Perugian school were military banners.

Churches were bastions and the lovely fountain of Giovanni Pisano served during numerous sieges as a reservoir rather than as an aesthetic object. After prolonged internal frays the town fell to the papacy, which constructed a citadel *ad coercendam Perusinorum audaciam*.

In the morning I had breakfast in a small bistro, cool as a cellar. Opposite sat a grey-haired man with a shaggy face, narrow eyes and the posture of a retired boxer. The picture of Hemingway. But as the proprietor proudly pointed out, it was Ezra Pound. The right man at the right place — an impetuous man who would feel at home in the company of the Baglionis.

In the middle of the fifteenth century, Piero della Francesca — a mature artist and, like his colleagues, a 'wandering performer' — travelled to Rome to paint the chambers of Pope Pius II. On his way he rested in Perugia. His polyptych, *Madonna and Child with Four Saints*, remains in the Pinacoteca. Its astonishing golden background is the apogee of Quattrocento. Piero painted the saints in abstract glory, rather than against a landscape, to suit the conservative, eternal taste of the brethren of S. Antonio delle Monache. Though it is not Piero's best work, it displays his characteristic tautness of human form with solid heads and shoulders like tree-tops. Most astonishing is the predella portraying St Francis receiving the stigmata — a direct reference to the tradition of Giotto. Two monks in an ashen, desert landscape with a Byzantine bird above — Christ.

Arezzo lies halfway between Perugia and Florence. A town that clings to a hill capped by a citadel. Here Petrarch was born — the son of a Florentine exile — who later discovered the country of exiles: philosophy. Here was born Aretino 'whose language hurt the living and the dead and who spared only God, explaining that he did not know him'.

St Francis's church is dark and austere. You must walk the length of an immense, unlit vestibule to reach the organ-loft and one of painting's greatest wonders: *The Legend of the True Cross*, a sequence of fourteen frescoes painted by Piero in full maturity between 1452 and 1466. The subject is derived from the apocryphal gospel of Nicodemus and Jacobus de Voragine's *Golden Legend*. Let us try to describe the fresco.

The Death of Adam. According to legend, the tree of the Cross grew from the seed placed under the tongue of the dying Father of

All Living. Naked Adam expires in the arms of aged Eve. Piero's elders are unlike those ruins so willingly painted by Rembrandt. They possess the pathos and wisdom of dying animals. Eve asks Seth to return to the Garden of Eden to bring an olive which will cure Adam. On the left, Seth talks with an angel in front of the Gate of Paradise. Adam lies in the centre — lifeless under a bare tree as he receives the seed from Seth. Figures bend their heads over the corpse. A woman with outspread arms cries voicelessly. Her lamentation carries not terror but prophesy. The entire scene appears Hellenic, as though the Old Testament were composed by Aeschylus.

The Queen of Sheba's Visit to Solomon. A medieval tale relates that the tree of the Cross survived until Solomon. The King ordered that it be felled and used for a bridge over the river Siloam. Here the Queen of Sheba surrounded by her maids experienced a vision and fell to her knees. Piero depicted human form as a supreme master. His figures are as unmistakable as the women in Botticelli. Piero's models have oval-shaped heads set on long, warm necks and full, strong shoulders. Their heads are accentuated by hair closely moulded to the skull. Their faces are bare — all life concentrated in the eyes, features tensed. Eyes with almond-shaped lids almost never return a glance. Piero avoids the cheap psychology of theatrical gestures and airs. When he wishes to stage a drama (as in the Queen of Sheba's lonely vision), he surrounds his heroine with a group of surprised girls. For greater contrast, he adds horses under a tree and two henchmen who prefer hooves and manes to miracles. As in other works, the time of day is indefinite: a pink-blue dawn or noon.

The scene continues as Piero holds the story through a unified perspective similar to the conventional unity of place in classical theatre. Under a Corinthian portico, drawn with architectural precision, the Queen of Sheba meets Solomon. Two worlds: the feminine court of the Queen, colourful and histrionic; and Solomon's officers, a study of severe political wisdom and serenity. There is the Renaissance variety of dress, but without Pisanello's ornament and detail. Solomon's men stand firmly on the stone floor; their long feet, seen in profile, recall Egyptian painting.

The bridge is dismantled in the next scene. Three workers carry a heavy log as though anticipating Christ's path to Golgotha. Yet this fragment (with the exception of the central figure) is so weighted and painted in a naïve manner that art historians detect the hand of Piero's disciples.

The Annunciation accords with an Albertian architecture of perfect balance and perspective. The austerity of marble conveys the gravity of discourse. A massive God the Father in a cloud with an angel on the left side; and Mary, a calm, sculpted Renaissance figure.

The Dream of Constantine. Piero leaves the stone porticoes and paints the golden-brown interior of Constantine's tent, one of the first conscious chiaroscuro nocturnes in Italian art. The torches' glow gently chisels the forms of two guardsmen, with a seated courtier and the sleeping Emperor in the foreground.

Constantine's Victory Over Maxentius evokes both Uccello and Velázquez, though Piero applies a classical simplicity and loftiness. Even the chaos of the cavalcade is organized. He never uses foreshortening for exclamation, never disturbs the harmony of planes. Raised lances support the morning sky, the landscape rains light.

The Torture of Judas portrays Judas, who was thrown into a dry well by order of Helena, the Emperor's mother, for not divulging the hiding place of the tree of the Cross. The scene depicts two servants lifting a repentant Judas from the well with a pulley attached to triangular scaffolding. Seneschal Boniface holds him tightly by the hair. Though the subject suggests a study of cruelty, Piero speaks in a sober, objective voice. The faces of the *dramatis personae* are unmoved and inattentive. If anything appears ominous, it is the apparatus which binds the convict. Once more geometry has absorbed passion.

The Discovery and Proof of the Cross. The fresco is divided into two sections which form an inseparable thematic and compositional unity. The first shows the excavation of the three crosses by workers watched by Constantine's mother. A medieval town of spires, slanted roofs, with pink and yellow walls rests in the distant valley. In the second section a half-naked man touched by the Cross rises from the dead. The Emperor's mother and her maids-of-honour worship the scene. The architectural background comments on the event. It is not the phantom medieval town of the previous scene, but a harmony of marble triangles, squares and circles: the mature wisdom of the Renaissance. The architecture is the final, rational confirmation of the miracle.

Thirty years after the discovery of the True Cross, the Persian King Chosroes captured Jerusalem and Christianity's most precious relic. In turn, the Persians were defeated by Emperor Heraclius. Piero unfolds the raging battle in a confused knot of men, horses and war implements which only superficially resembles the famous battles of Uccello. Uccello's conflicts are loud. Copper horses stamp their hind legs, the massacre's uproar rises to the sheet-iron sky and falls heavily to earth. In Piero all the gestures are slow, solemn. His narration conveys and epic impassiveness as both sides conduct their bloody rites with the earnestness of lumbermen felling a forest. The sky above the contestants is transparent. In the wind the banners 'bow their wings like dragons, lizards and birds pierced with spears'.

Finally, the victorious, barefoot Heraclius carries the Cross to Jerusalem, leading a ceremonial procession of Greek and Armenian priests with their colourful, bizarre head-dresses. Art historians wonder where Piero could have observed such fantastic costumes. Perhaps they were introduced for the sake of composition. With his taste for the monumental, Piero crowns the heads of his figures like an architect captitalizing columns. Heraclius's procession, the finale of the *Golden Legend*, resounds with a pure, dignified note.

Piero's masterpiece has been severely damaged by damp and a restorer's incompetence. The colours are faded as though rubbed with flour, and the poor lighting of the organ-loft hinders contemplation. Yet, if only one legendary figure remained, one piece of wood, one splinter of sky, we could reconstruct from these scraps the whole, like the fragments of a Greek temple.

The key to Piero's mystery: he was one of the most impersonal, supra-individual artists in history. Berenson compares him to the anonymous sculptor of the Parthenon and to Velázquez. His human figures enact the grave drama of demigods, heroes and giants. The absence of psychological expression unveils the pure artistic movement within mass and light. 'Facial expression is so unnecessary and sometimes so embarrassing that I often prefer a statue without a head,' confesses Berenson. Malraux welcomes Piero as the inventor of indifference: 'His sculpted crowd comes alive only during a sacred dance . . . which reflects the principle of contemporary sensitivity. Expression should come from the painting not from the depicted forms.' Over the battle of shadows, convulsions and tumult, Piero has erected *lucidus ordo* — an eternal order of light and balance.

I thought that I might spare Monterchi, a small village twenty-five kilometres from Arezzo. A pond of stones covered by cypress trees and blue skies — like duckweed. But I was swayed by a friend's letter: 'The cemetery and chapel are situated on a hill some hundred metres from the village in which a strange car is a sensational event. It is reached through rows of olive trees that pave the vineyards. The chapel and caretaker's house stand in line with the tombs and take their pastoral appearance from the rich vine vegetation. Girls and mothers with children come here for their evening strolls.'

Outside the chapel is yellow, inside lime-white; perhaps baroque but really deprived of style. It is minute, with the altar's *mensa* situated in a niche. There is hardly enough room for a coffin and a few mourners. The walls are bare, with the sole ornament a framed, transposed fresco damaged at the sides and bottom. In their journey through the ages, the fresco's angels have lost their sandals, though some clumsy restorer has tried to replace them.

It is certainly one of painting's most provocative Madonnas. Her hair, pressed to her skull, uncovers large ears. She has a sensual neck and full arms, a straight nose and a hard, swollen mouth. Her eyes are lowered, her eyelids drawn over black pupils which stare into her body. She wears a simple, high-waisted dress open from breast to knees. Her left hand rests on a hip, a country bridesmaid's gesture; the right hand touches her belly but without a trace of licentiousness, as though touching a mystery. Piero has painted for the Monterchi peasants the tender, eternal secret of every mother. Two angels briskly draw aside the drapery like a stage curtain.

It was fortunate that Piero was born neither in Florence nor Rome — but in small Borgo San Sepolcro, far from the tumults of history. For he would often return to his gentle, native town, would hold municipal office and die here.

Palazzo Comunale retains two works by its greatest son. Focillon considers the polyptych *The Madonna of the Misericordia* Piero's first unassisted painting. The upper part depicts the Crucifixion. Christ is seen in a tragic and stern posture; but at the foot of the Cross, Mary and St John possess an emotive force unusual in Piero's later work. The gestures of their arms and spread fingers portray a violent despair without Piero's poetry of reserve and silence. The seed of his future style is revealed in the main painting: the Madonna shielding the faithful with her robe. As the central figure, she is tall, strong and impersonal — an elemental form. Her grey-green robe flows like warm rain down upon the heads of the kneeling believers.

The Resurrection of Christ was painted with the sure hand of a forty-year-old man. Christ stands firmly against a melancholy

Tuscan landscape. A victorious figure. He holds a banner in his left hand while the other hand clasps the shroud which is like a senator's toga. He has a wise, wild face with the deep eyes of Dionysus. He rests his right foot on the edge of the tomb like someone crushing the neck of an enemy defeated in a duel. In the foreground, four Roman guards are paralysed by sleep. The two contrasted states are striking: the sudden awakening against the heavy slumber of men turned into objects. The sky and Christ are drawn with light; the guards and the background landscape are darkened. Though the figures appear static, Piero with a stroke of genius reconciles disorder and movement, energy and torpidity: the drama of life and death measured by inertia.

Urbino has been compared to a lady seated on a black throne covered with a green mantle. The lady is a palace dominating the small town just as its owners, the Montefeltro dukes, dominated its history.

They began as robber knights. Dante — an expert on last things — placed one of them, Guido, in an infernal circle occupied by the moaning sowers of discord. Gradually, their tempers cooled, and their dispositions became more gentle. Federigo, whose rule began in 1444, was the example of a humanist general. If he engaged in wars, as for instance against the ruthless Malatesta of Rimini who murdered two wives (shown by Piero piously kneeling in front of S. Sigismondo), he entered the arena with an obvious distaste for the blood sport. He was both valiant and prudent. Through his *condottiere* service for the Sforzi, the Aragons and the Pope, he tripled his domain. He liked to walk alone, unguarded (a practised propaganda trick) in a simple, red vestment and talk with his subjects in the duchy's capital. Though subjects had to kneel and kiss his hand during these friendly chats, Federigo was considered a liberal ruler for his time.

His court, renowned for its unusual moral purity, was the shelter of humanists. He was the model for Castiglione's *The Courtier*. The Duke collected antiques, artists and scholars. He maintained close contacts with Alberti, the most prominent architect of the age, the sculptor Rossellino, and the masters Joos van Gent, Piero and Melozzo da Forli — in whose portrait the Duke sits in his library in full armour (but this junk is only the embellishment of power) grasping a huge volume set on a book-rest. A book-lover of the highest standard, Federigo demanded a Hebrew Bible as ransom after the Battle of Volterra. His library of rare theological and humanistic manuscripts was certainly richer than his armoury.

We mention Federigo da Montefeltro since for many years he was Piero della Francesca's friend and protector, which should entitle a posthumous fame. Perhaps Piero spent his most enjoyable years here. Vasari, an important source for lost masterpieces, says that Piero painted in Urbino a sequence of small pictures that were greatly to the Duke's liking, though they have disappeared during the wars which ravished the land.

Piero's diptych of Federigo and his wife, Battista Sforza, resides in the Uffizi Gallery in Florence. A striking contrast exists between the two figures. Battista's face is waxen, drained of blood (thus the speculation that the portrait was painted after her death), while the Duke's tawny face vibrates with energy: a hawkish profile — a head with raven-black hair set on a lion's neck, a strong torso in a robe and red head-dress. Duke Montefeltro's bust rises like a lone rock against a remote and delicately painted landscape. Our sight must span an abyss — without any intermediate planes, without the continuity of space and perspective. The figure of the Duke falls from an ineffably light sky like a hot meteor.

On the portrait's reverse are two allegorical scenes full of courtly poetry. They depict the triumphal processions popular in Renaissance painting. Surrounded by the four theological virtues, the coach of the Duchess is drawn by four unicorns. The dimmed, grey landscape brightens at the infinite horizon's line — an evocation of death.

The Duke's coach is drawn by white stallions. Federigo is accompanied by Justice, Power and Moderation. A fantastic mountain landscape radiates light. A blue afterglow is reflected in the water's mirror. The allegory's inscription proclaims:

> *Clarus insigni vehitur triumpho*
> *Quem parem summis ducibus perhennis*
> *Fame virtutem celebrat decenter*
> *Sceptra tenentem*

The gallery in Urbino contains two masterpieces from separate periods of Piero's life. *Senigallia*, named after the church where it previously hung, portrays the Madonna with two angels. Despite the lack of evidence, it is considered one of Piero's last works. Though some see signs of senile decadence, it is difficult to agree with that judgement. One rather concurs with those who discover an attempted rejuvenation of style.

The new light came from the North. *Senigallia* best conveys the dramatic encounter between the Italian master's imagination and the power of Van Eyck, to whom Piero turned in his youth. This influence is confirmed by Piero's unusual devotion to detail. The hands of the angels, Madonna and Child are painted with a typically Flemish love of detail. The scene is placed in a private interior (an exception for Piero). We see a fragment of a grey-blue chamber opening to a corridor on the right side. The corridor's perspective is discontinued; it stops abruptly at a slanted wall with windows. The penetrating light does not reach the foreground figures. It is a chiaroscuro study. Human forms are succinct and monumental. The Madonna has the common face of a nurse, the foster-mother of kings. Little Jesus raises his hand in a lordly manner and looks straight ahead with his wise, severe eyes — the diminished figure of the future emperor aware of his power and fate.

The Flagellation of Christ surprises us with its original treatment of subject and perfect harmony of composition, a synthesis of painting and architecture as yet unseen in European art. We have often repeated the term 'monumental', to indicate the presence of architecture in Piero's work. We must look more closely at this relation, since the loss of architectural sense, the highest art organizing the visible, is the drama of contemporary painting.

The man who influenced Piero more than any painter (Domenico Veneziano, Sassetta, Van Eyck, his contemporary perspectivists: Uccello and Masaccio) was an architect, Leon Battista Alberti.

Born in Genoa in 1404, he came from a prominent, banished Florentine family whose importance can be expressed in a figure: the high price offered to slay its members by the vengeful Albizzis. Leon Battista received a truly Renaissance education in Bologna while living in student poverty after his father's death. He took his doctorate in law and studied Greek, mathematics, music and architecture, which were complemented by his travels. His fortune changed frequently, only improving when his humanist friend, Tommaso da Sarzana, became Pope Nicolas V. Alberti was praised equally for his beauty and intellectual virtues, an example of a Renaissance athlete and encyclopedic mind, 'a man of outstanding mind, acute judgement and thorough knowledge'.

This is how Angelo Poliziano introduced him to Lorenzo de'

Medici: 'Neither the oldest books nor the most unusual skills are unknown to this man. You can only wonder whether he is more gifted in rhetoric or poetry, whether his style is more solemn or elegant. He has studied the remains of ancient buildings so thoroughly that he has mastered the oldest ways of building while imparting these methods to his contemporaries. He has invented machines and constructed beautiful buildings; besides, he is considered an outstanding painter and sculptor.' His last years (he died in Rome in 1472) were irradiated with fame. He was a friend of the Gonzagas and Medicis.

He left nearly fifty works: studies, dissertations, dialogues and moral treatises not counting numerous letters and apocryphal writings. His lasting fame rests upon his works on sculpture, painting and architecture. His main treatise, *De Re Aedificatoria*, is by no means a manual for engineers but a charming, learned book for art patrons and humanists. Despite its classical structure, technical subjects are mixed with anecdotes and trivia. We may read about foundations, building-sites, bricklaying, doorknobs, wheels, axes, levers, hacks, and how to 'exterminate and destroy snakes, mosquitoes, bed-bugs, flies, fleas, mice, moths and other importunate night creatures'. Alberti's treatise on painting written in 1435, directly influenced Piero. In the introduction the author warns that he will not tell stories about painters since he wishes to construct the art of painting *ab ovo*.

Many sources claim that Renaissance artists were satisfied with mere imitation of classical styles and nature. Alberti's writings demonstrate that matters were not so simple. He states that the artist, even more than the philosopher, is the architect of the world. Though he may borrow from certain natural relationships, proportions and rules, his discovery is through his vision rather than mathematical speculation. 'What cannot be perceived by the eye is without interest for the painter.' The eye's image is a combination of rays which thread the object to the spectator in constructing a visual pyramid. Painting cuts through this visual prism. The result is a definite, operational chain based upon the logic of sight. One must locate the object in space and enclose it within a linear contour. Then the harmonized surfaces become the colour composition.

Differences in colour issue from differences in lighting. Before Alberti, painters used colour. (Renaissance theoreticians often sneered at the chromatic chaos of the Middle Ages.) After Alberti, they played with light. The stress placed upon colour makes it impossible to define form by a sharp contour. Piero understood this lesson. He concentrates on an object's inner space rather than its outline. Seth's nakedness or the Queen of Sheba's head are surrounded by a luminescent lining like the edges of clouds. This bright contour is Alberti's theory in practice.

A painting's composition unifies objects and space. The narration can be reduced to figures, figures dismembered into elements, elements into adjoining surfaces like the facets of a diamond. However, this should not lead to a geometrical coldness. Venturi has observed that Piero's compositional forms aspire toward geometry without entering Plato's paradise of cones, spheres and cubes. He is, to use an anachronism, like a figurative painter who has passed through a cubist phase.

Alberti is attentive to narrative painting, though he declares that an image should act upon itself and charm the spectator regardless of plot. Emotion should be released through the movements of bodies and forms rather than facial expression. He warns against tumult, lushness and detail. This warning became the two rules governing Pierro's most outstanding compositions: the harmonized background and the principle of tranquillity.

In his best paintings (*The Nativity*, the portrait of the Duke of Urbino, *The Baptism, Constantine's Victory*) the remote, absorbent background is as significant as his figures. The contrast between the massive human shapes (usually seen from below) and the delicate landscape attenuates the drama of man in space. The landscapes are deserted, with only the elements of water, earth and sky. The quiet chanting of the air and the immense planes are the choir against which Piero's personae remain silent.

The principle of tranquillity does not reside merely in architectural balance. It is a principle of inner order. Piero understood that excess movement and expression both destroy the visual painted space and compress time to a momentary scene, the flesh of existence. His stoic heroes are constrained and impassive. The stilled leaves, the hue of the first earthly dawn, the unstruck hour present Piero's creations in their eternal armour.

Let us return to *The Flagellation*. It is Piero's most Albertian work. The compositional threads are cool, taut and balanced. Each person stands in an exact construction like a rock of ice, which at first glance seems under the rule of the demon of perspective.

The scene is divided into two parts. The main drama occurs on the left side under a marble portico supported by Corinthian columns where pure intelligence could walk. The rectangular floor tiles guide our sight toward the semi-robed Christ. He leans against a column on which rests the stone statue of a Greek hero with a raised hand. Two henchmen simultaneously lift their whips. Their strokes will be regular and indifferent like the ticking of a clock. The silence is complete, without the victim's moans or the executioners' odious breath. There are two observers: one turned away; the other seated showing his left-side profile. Were only this section to remain, it would be a box scene — a model sealed in glass, tamed reality. Knowing that geometry devours passion, Piero never placed important events in perspective (unlike the ironist Breughel, *vide Icarus*). The significant figures of his dramas stand in the foreground as if in front of footlights. The picture's symbolic meaning is thus associated with the three men standing at the right with their backs turned to the martyr.

Berenson and Malraux were interested only in their compositional function. 'In order to make this scene even more severe and cruelly impersonal, the artist introduced three magnificent forms which stand in the foreground like eternal rocks.' Traditional interpretation connects this work to a contemporary historical event: the violent death of Duke Oddantonio da Montefeltro, here surrounded by two conspirators. Behind their backs, murderous intentions are realized by the symbolic whipping. Suarez gives reign to his imagination and plunges into a risky explanation: the three mysterious men are the high priest of the Temple of Jerusalem, the Roman proconsul and a pharisee. Turning their backs to the momentous event, they consider its significance and consequences. In their cyphered faces Suarez sees three different states: the pharisee's restrained hatred, the Roman bureaucrat's stubborn righteousness, and the priest's cynical peace. Whatever key we may use, *The Flagellation* will remain one of the world's most closed and obscure paintings. We view it through a thin pane of ice — chained, fascinated and helpless as in a dream.

Madonna and Child with Saints and Angels is claimed to be Piero's last painting. Though its authorship was the subject of controversy, it now rests with Piero's name in Milan's Brera Gallery. Ten figures surround the Madonna in a half-circle, ten columns of flesh and blood with the rhythm repeated in the background architecture. The scene is situated in an apse with a full arch and a cone-shaped vault opening above. From the top of the cone an egg hangs on a thin line. This may seem a trivial description but the unexpected, formal element is surprisingly logical and correct. The painting is Piero's testament. And an egg, as we know, used to symbolize the secret of life. Under the mature vault, this fixed pendulum on a straight line will strike for Piero della Francesca the hour of immortality.

Was the greatness of his art equally obvious to his contemporaries and descendants as it is for us? Piero was a recognized artist though he worked very slowly and did not achieve the fame of his colleagues in Florence. He was praised mainly for his two theoretical works written at the end of his life. It comes as no surprise that he was quoted more frequently by architects than by painters or poets. Cillenio devotes one sonnet to Piero; Giovanni Santi, Raphael's father, mentions him in his rhymed chronicle; another poet alludes to the portrait of Federigo da Montefeltro. Not much.

Vasari, born nineteen years after Piero's death, adds only a few biographical details. He stresses his expression, realism and passion for detail, which is a clear misunderstanding. Later, chroniclers and art historians issue a dispassionate drone of quotations from his work.

In the seventeenth and eighteenth centuries, Piero's fame subsided. His name was buried as art pilgrimages streamed from Florence to Rome leaving aside Arezzo, not to mention tiny Borgo San Sepolcro. No one knows whether the large quantity of wine consumed or the taste of the epoch was responsible for the unfavourable insinuation in von Rumohr's *Italienische Forschungen* that the painter called Piero della Francesca was not worth mentioning. His rehabilitation was left until the middle of the nineteenth century. Stendhal (not the first case in which a writer precedes the discoveries of art historians) saved him from oblivion. He compared him to Uccello and stressed his masterful perspective, his synthesis of architecture and painting; but as if swayed by Vasari's judgement, he says: '*Toute la beauté est dans l'expression.*' Piero's place amongst the greatest European painters was restored by Crowe and Cavalcaselle in their *History of Painting in Italy*, published in England in the years 1864–66. Later, the studies start to flow: from Berenson to Roberto Longhi, Piero's exquisite monographist. Malraux says that the present century has rendered justice to four artists: Georges de la Tour, Vermeer, El Greco and Piero.

What do we know about his life? Nothing or almost nothing.

Even the date of his birth is uncertain (1410–1420?). He was the son of the artisan Benedetto di Franceschi and Romana di Perino da Monterchi. His academy was Domenico Veneziano's studio in Florence though he did not remain long. He probably felt most at home in his little Borgo San Sepolcro. He worked consecutively in Ferrara, Rimini, Rome, Arezzo and Urbino. In 1450 he fled from the plague to Bastia; in Rimini he bought a house with a garden; in 1486 he signed his will. He shared his experience not only with his disciples, for he left two theoretical treatises: *De Quinque Corporibus Regolaribus* and *De Prospettiva Pingendi*, in which he discussed optics and perspective in a precise, scientific manner. He died on 12 October 1492.

It is impossible to place him in a romance. He hides so thoroughly behind his paintings and frescoes that one cannot invent his private life, his loves and friendships, his ambitions, his passion and grief. He has received the greatest act of mercy by absent-minded history, which mislays documents and blurs all traces of life. If he still endures, it is not through anecdotes of the miseries of his life, his madness, his successes and failures. His entire being is in his *œuvre*.

I imagine him walking along a narrow San Sepolcro street towards the town gate, with only the cemetery and the Umbrian hills beyond. He wears a grey robe over his broad shoulders. He is short, stocky, strolling with a peasant's assurance. He silently returns salutations.

Tradition holds that he went blind towards the end of his life. Marco di Longara told Berto degli Alberti that as a young boy he walked the streets of Borgo San Sepolcro with an old, blind painter called Piero della Francesca.

Little Marco could not have known that his hand was leading light.

MEMORIES OF VALOIS

Adieu Paris. Nous cherchons l'amour, le bonheur, l'innocence. Nous ne serons jamais assez loin de toi.

I DO not know why Poles, a naturally mobile nation encouraged by history to excessive dislocation, embrace Paris in a trance. The city is unquestionably beautiful, but the true France has moved beyond its gates.

After the customary excursions to Chartres and Versailles, it is proper to visit the charming towns and villages scattered within a hundred kilometres — M. Hulot's auto can reach them in an hour and a half. The chain of the most gracious Gothic cathedrals: Morienval or St Loup-du-Naud for those who want Romanesque without travelling to Burgundy or Provence; the ruins of Les Andelys; the palaces of Compiègne, Fontainebleau, Rambouillet; and the forests, the wonderful forests where one can still hear the call of history.

North of Paris — Valois — old France. The heritage of Clovis, King of the Franks. Once the country's most valuable domain. Twice ruled by the king's brothers; twice by princes of Valois. The land 'where the heart of France has been beating for more than a thousand years'.

Chantilly

Chantilly is situated among forests near the Nonette, a river named like a girl from a fairy-tale. A well-fed town with a palace, upper-class villas and a famous race-course. I am here for the third time. This time to visit Sassetta, for whom one must cross the entire town.

The houses are clean and rich. They glitter like a copper name-

163

plate, the token of a notary's affluence. The hour is early. The shutters are closed, the wicket-gates shut, the gardens divided neatly and jealously by fences, like feudal domains. Over a low wall, you can see a vassal in blue trousers mowing the lawn.

The most frequent word here is 'private': a private road, private property, private wells, private passage, private meadow. On a carefully mown meadow protected by a fence, a scene from Degas: four couples waltzing on horseback, practising complicated figures. No, they are not a circus troupe. Their performance is more dignified and thus slightly boring: in pairs, then single file, a lady to the right, a man to the left, then a circle. What right have I to comment on these pleasures, when my only pitiful contact with a horse's back lasted a few minutes during a peasant feast. In any event, it seemed that I had touched on a distant epoch before reaching the palace of Chantilly.

On the way one must pass the Great Stables, a masterpiece of eighteenth-century architecture in the style of Louis XV. A huge, hoof-shaped building which once held two hundred and forty horses and four hundred and twenty hounds, not counting the entire army of stable boys, equerries, dog-keepers and veterinary surgeons. After the stables, the palace is much less impressive. Erected in the 'Renaissance' style it has an added 'Gothic' chapel whose falsity can be felt from a distance.

Two thousand years ago Chantilly was the site of Cantilius, a Gallo-Roman stronghold. In the Middle Ages, it was the home of '*le bouteiller de France*' who cared for the royal cellars and had the ear of the king. In the fourteenth century, Chancellor Orgemont built a castle, which through marriages fell to the barons of Montmorency who were warlords and councillors related to the royal family. One member, Anne de Montmorency, thrust his way into history — a magnificent figure of a knight, diplomat and councillor to five consecutive French kings, from Louis XII to Charles IX. He commanded more than a hundred castles, an astronomical fortune, immense political influence and an indestructable body. He expired at the age of seventy-five in battle against the Protestants at Saint-Denis, after five sword wounds, two head blows from a battle-axe and a harquebus shot (falling, he broke the pommel of his sword with his jaw).

Chantilly occupies an important niche in France's sentimental history as the scene of the last great love of Vert-Galant, that is Henry IV. He fell in love with Caroline de Montmorency, the daughter of his friend and host. The beautiful girl possessed Lolita's maturity while His Grace could count fifty-four years. As a shrewd politician he matched Caroline with Henry II Bourbon-Condé who was timid, clumsy and dim-witted. In a word, the antithesis of Vert-Galant. Though the intrigue was clear, fate was capricious since the young couple escaped from Chantilly to Brussels, under the protection of the King of Spain. Henry IV raged to the point of asking the Pope's assistance in this rather mundane matter. However, Ravaillac's stiletto quickly pacified the royal heart.

Though the present palace is a poor imitation, its surroundings compensate for its architectural faults: the park, the wood, the wide, green moat filled with voracious carp whose open mouths evoke hunger even in an ascetic. Yet France cannot boast an abundance of gastronomic ascetics. Chantilly is connected with Vatel who made history as a glutton and gourmet. The story began on the 23 April 1671, when King Louis XIV and his court came to the great Condé's residence at Chantilly. The immense assembly of five thousand people demanded an army of servants and cooks. Its commander was Vatel, '*contrôleur général de la Bouche de Monsieur le Prince*'. After a smooth start, two of the sixty tables ran short of meat. Vatel could not bear the humiliation and stabbed himself with his sword. Madame de Sévigné tells the story with taste and emotion.

The Chantilly Gallery can match the Louvre, though the schools and epochs are cast in an odd mixture. The princes (out of sheer absent-mindedness, one presumes) have inserted unbelievable nineteenth-century duds among the masterpieces. However without this collection our knowledge of French painting, especially from the fifteenth and sixteenth centuries, would be incomplete. We might mention the portraits of Corneille de Lyon, a rich collection of drawings and paintings by Jean and François Clouet, Etienne Chevalier's *Book of Hours* illustrated by Jean Fouquet, and one of the world's most magnificent illustrated manuscripts, *Les très riches heures du Duc de Berry*.

To view and experience miniature paintings demands a special disposition and talent. One must enter a world enclosed like a glass sphere. Our situation resembles Alice's in Wonderland, who opens a door with a golden key and sees the most beautiful garden, though it be too small to enter. 'Oh, if one could fold up like a telescope.' Looking at miniatures is for those who can fold up. History saved only the first names of the illustrators: Pol, Jean and Herman. We know that they came from Limbourg, that is from Flanders, which in the fifteenth century belonged to the powerful, art-loving Burgundy princes.

We have said that *Les très riches heures* are miniatures, which is a precise cataloguer's phrase. Their artistry has another origin. We touch upon the point at which painting leaves the pages of manuscript, and gives birth to canvases. It is not enough to tear a page from a book and hang it on the wall. The gesture must be preceded by the miniature's intrinsic evolution. Colour must acquire the intensity to express the material mutability of the world. The image must radiate its own light independent of surroundings and attain a definite boundary and depth. In a word, it must attire an ontological body — leave the stage of simple beings and reach the realm of complex structures. The Limbourg brothers' miniatures foreshadow the breakthrough. The linear perspective is naïve and awkward in a charming way, but the space built with colour is so convincing that our sight flows inward.

July. Sheep-shearing in a lush green foreground. Our gaze travels over a yellow oblong of grain; a jump across the river collides with the hard, pearly wall of a castle with its deep-blue roof. Beyond the cone-shaped mountains and golden hills — the blue eye of infinity.

The landscape is a partner, a character in a scene, not decoration. The Limbourg brothers' love of detail is striking. Tillage under the signs of Scorpio and Libra. Neatly divided ridges woven like tresses. In the ridges crows searching for worms. Yet the picture is no larger than a hand — with the further addition of a castle and its towers. The worms remain unrepresented, which undoubtedly troubled the Flemish painters' hunger for truth.

But Sassetta, where is Sassetta, I came here for Sassetta. What a pleasure to find one's 'own' painting in the right place. It is small, almost totally subdued by the surrounding canvases. It is titled *The Betrothal of St Francis to Poverty*. Two monks (St Francis with an aureole) face three slim girls: in grey, green and purple. There is a subtle gesture like the spinning of a delicate thread between the hands of the saint and the middle figure. Above, the three mystical girls calmly fly away with only the backward bend of their feet conveying their flight. A white stone castle to the right is so light that a butterfly could capture it. The Tuscan landscape — grey and green as evening approaches. Tree-tops are placed separately in the landscape like notes. The sky descends in stripes as in oriental paintings

— cool blue at the top with a weightless, limitless luminescence hovering above the gently modulated hills.

Sassetta's painting is scandalously anachronistic if judged on style. The artist seems blind to 'the new'. He lives in the middle of the Quattrocento, yet he paints as if it were the thirteenth century. He builds a human body of vegetable fibre without flesh and bones as suits the age of Masaccio and Donatello. His contempt for the laws of gravitation is complete; and his tender, linear composition places him closer to the Byzantines than any Florentine or Venetian painter. Yet it is difficult to leave Sassetta, whose paintings radiate an irresistable charm, without redefining our vision. Fortunately, art history differs from a geometry textbook for it can accommodate artists of charm: Sano di Pietro from Siena, Baldovinetti from Florence or the Venetian, Carpaccio.

Huge stairs lead from the palace to a logical French garden encircled by the Avenue of Philosophers where the prince's guests once walked: Bossuet (his speech at the great Condé's funeral is still a student's nightmare, but what an oration!), Fénelon, Bourdaloue, La Bruyère (teacher of the prince's grandson), Molière (he owed the production of *Tartuffe* to patronage), Boileau, Racine, La Fontaine, and the ladies, de La Fayette and de Sévigné — in a word, an anthology of seventeenth-century French literature. Beyond the Avenue of Philosophers, an exuberant English garden with winding paths, thick bushes — a distinct lack of veneration for the classical rules — with delightful cascades, islands of love and miniature villages with mills and cottages in which the elegant company disguised as peasants ate sumptuous meals.

As the Senlis bus enters the forest, one may glimpse the palace in the green frame of the water's reflection. It appears suddenly, as though lit by lightning.

Senlis

> Who invented that abyss and cast it upwards?
> JULIAN PRZYBOŚ

> Tomorrow, the archers of Senlis must give
> back the bouquet to those of Loisy.
>
> *Sylvie*

History has passed through Senlis. It has lived within its walls for centuries, then departed. What remains is an arena overgrown with grass, a broken circle of Gallo-Roman walls besieged by vine, bits of a royal palace, the Abbey of St Victor converted to a noisy dormitory, and a cathedral, one of the oldest cathedrals in the great Ile-de-France Gothic chain.

Yet Senlis is not a sad town, not a desperately sad town like a crown excavated from a tomb. It is an old, silver coin with the image of a harsh emperor, which you can safely turn in your fingers like a nut. It rests on a small hill in the company of eternal forests encircled by the Nonette.

We have said that Senlis Cathedral is one of the oldest Gothic churches. This requires further explanation since in this case chronology is misleading. The founder of Gothic was Suger, a minister and royal regent of France. When appointed abbot of the coronation cathedral of Saint-Denis (now in a working class Paris suburb), he reconstructed the old, Carolingian church widening its portals and organ-loft and raising the vault. This was the first use of ogive and cross-ribbed vaulting, which for some scholars is the essence of Gothic style. On 19 January 1143, a hurricane raged above the town causing widespread destruction. Though still under construction, the cathedral remained intact. The pious considered it a miracle; the architects, proof of the design's sturdiness. A new epoch in the history of architecture commenced.

It is questionable whether the pointed arches which form an X in the cross-ribbed vault (its invention wrongly attributed to the cathedral builders) are as structurally significant as Viollet-le-Duc, Choisy and Lasterrie deemed. An hypothesis that this vaulting was mere ornament was prompted by the research of the engineer Sabouret and the architect Pol Abraham, who studied the cathedrals bombed in 1914 and tested the old materials. The problem is not so simple. Moreover, the aesthetic-minded historians of architecture stress style — a completely new system of Gothic proportions — rather than construction.

A popular view is that a new order appears as the old withers. This biological theory does not apply to Gothic replacing the Romanesque. When Gothic appeared in the middle of the twelfth century, the Romanesque did not display any shades of decline. Its displacement was not motivated by the desire to build larger churches since Vézelay Cathedral is nearly as large as Notre-Dame. The general plan of cathedrals remained almost unchanged. Some historians connect the birth of Gothic with the political expansion of the Capetians as the struggle between the spirits of the North and South culminated in the bloody crusade against the Albigensians. The emergence of Gothic accorded with the new spiritual attitude. The condensed, contemplative Romanesque cathedrals were opposed by dynamic, restless edifices in which light, 'the divine essence', harnessed the leading role. This coincided with Suger's love of splendour, the opulence of interiors and stained glass — new constellations of precious stones revealed by a thousand burning candles.

Suger is a vivid, fascinating figure. A servant's son, politician, organizer and builder, a friend of kings — his religious habit covers powerful passions.. Many were offended by his insatiable love of glamour. When he writes about gold, crystals, amethysts, rubies and emeralds — unexpected presents from three abbots for the inlay of his crucifix — one feels that his eyes burn with a very mundane glow. Modesty was not among his virtues. He ordered the abbey's treasury to set aside funds for his funeral celebrations, previously a royal privilege. Thirteen inscriptions in the cathedral praise his merits. We see him in stained glass at Our Lady's feet, his legs piously bent but his hands active. Moreover, his name is written as large as the Virgin's. Suger was a refined writer with a brilliant mind. His connections with neo-Platonic philosophy are indisputable. His conduct scandalized St Bernard of Clairvaux, a member of the rigid Cistercian branch of the Benedictines. The dispute between these two church powers is as fascinating as the controversy between the classicists and the romantics.

However, the reconstruction of the abbey of Saint-Denis was not solely a matter of personal ambition and taste; it was a necessity. With the vividness of a nineteenth-century writer, he describes a holiday in the basilica:

'One could see the most outrageous sights: the backward pressure of the thick human mass against those who still wanted to enter to pay homage and kiss the holy relics, the Nail and Crown of Our Lord, was so great that none of the many thousands could move for the unusual compression of bodies. One could do nothing but stay immobilized like a marble statue or utter a cry. The terror of the women was great and unbearable; suffering in the mass of strong men, squeezed like a press, their faces were like bloodless signs of death; they cried terribly as if in labour; some were trampled mercilessly, others were carried by men who helped through pity; many barely managed to escape into the monastery's garden where, re-signed, they gasped for air. Sometimes the brothers who had been showing the tokens of Our Lord's passion, disgusted by their rage and quarrels, could do nothing better than to run away with the relics through the window.'

The consecration of Saint-Denis' new organ-loft commenced on the second Sunday of June, 1144. It was not only Suger's great day, but also a milestone in the history of architecture. The celebration was attended by the King and Queen, peers, archbishops and bishops. The latter were surely unable to sleep when returning to their gloomy churches at Chartres, Soissons, Reims, Beauvais or Senlis.

As early as 1153, Bishop Thibault of Senlis received a royal letter of recommendation for a new church urging money collectors to travel throughout France for contributions. The construction was slow, and its consecration in 1191 was held before the work was completed. In the middle of the thirteenth century a transverse nave was added, and the southern tower was topped with a magnificent spire. The flight of the eighty-metre tower is breathtaking. The façade is slender, austere and bare. The Senlis spire sways against the clouds like a tree. The anonymous architects have touched on the mystery of organic architecture.

A fire opened the path to regrettable restoration. The southern façade contrasts with the face of the cathedral. It is entwined with the tangled lines of flamboyant Gothic. Nothing can compete with the simple architecture of the thirteenth century; the capricious airs of the sixteenth century foretell a lethal exhaustion.

Three portals lead inside. The two tympanums carry a rare archi-tectural motif (columns and arches, abstract, without narration) while the one above the main entrance opens a new epoch in the history of iconography. In Senlis the theme of the Virgin Mary is introduced for the first time in place of the Romanesque 'Last Judgement' (Christ in majesty and a crowd of Apostles and saints), with the saved flying heavily into the sky as the damned are thrown into the abyss. The theme was continued in Chartres, Notre-Dame de Paris, in Reims and other cathedrals. The Virgin's sudden appear-ance in monumental Gothic sculpture seems a response to the love poetry of the troubadours, the praise of women, and the concept of courtly love which the Church wished to sublimate.

The death, resurrection and triumph of Mary is told with a powerful simplicity. The 'Resurrection' is most beautiful. Six angels lift Mary from her bed wrapped in a rough-textured cocoon. The angels are full-cheeked, young. They fulfill their duty with earnestness and flair, as though they carried school satchels instead of wings.

The call of Gothic is as irresistible as the call of mountains. One cannot remain a passive observer for long. These are not Romanesque cathedrals, where from barren vaults drops of consolation fall. A Gothic cathedral relates not only to eyes but also to muscles. Dizziness combines with aesthetic exaltation.

I start to climb the tower. At first, several rough steps form a path, but soon I enter the triforum's wide platform which appears to have been smitten by a stone avalanche: a disorder of masks, gargoyles and the split heads of saints. I am midway between the stone vault and the floor of the nave.

Further climbing is more difficult. The steps are obliterated, and one must search for hand-holds. Finally, I reach another platform, a narrow gallery just above the main portal. On both sides rest two summits — towers with slender, spiral peaks — which shadow the main nave like the shade of a mighty spruce.

Eight centuries have brought the cathedral close to nature. Patches of lichen, grass between the stones, and bright yellow flowers spring from the curves. A cathedral is like a mountain; no later style, neither Renaissance nor Classic, could retain the symbiosis between architecture and vegetation. The Gothic is natural.

And animals are here, too! From behind a ledge a huge lizard watches me with its protuding eyes. Monsters with dog-heads warm in the sun on inaccessible rock shoulders. For the moment the menagerie is asleep. But some day (perhaps Judgement Day) they will descend the stone stairs and enter the town.

The gallery is decorated with four figures: Adam, Eve and two saints. They have the charm of folk sculptures. Especially beautiful Eve. Coarse-grained, big-eyed and plump. A heavy plait of hair falls on her wide, warm back.

Time to be on my way. The end of an easy approach and the beginning of the ascent to the summit. It is a vertical crevasse. Sometimes I walk in total darkness clinging with both hands to the wall; sometimes the steps become loose stones. I must stop at shorter intervals to steady my breath. The rock wall is split by small windows which let in sudden, blinding flashes. Through a crack one can see clouds and the sky framed by darkness. I am high in a stone gorge which opens to heaven. The stairs end. In front there is a wall in which I must find a grip. If it were more slanted, it would be a typical overhang. I climb vertically, fighting for balance with my entire body. Finally an open platform — the end of the ascent. Blood pounds in my temples. I cling to a small stone niche. Below, an endless fall. Distant fields breathe gently. They float into my eyes like consent.

'With a trowel in his hand, the mason Abraham Knupfer sings while hanging in the air on scaffolding so high that, reading Gothic poems on a huge bell, he has at his feet a church of thirty tall arches and a town of thirty churches. He sees the stone gargoyles spew torrents of slate down the intricate chasm of galleries, windows, balconies, bell-towers, spires, roofs and wooden binders with the grey stain of a plucked, limp wing of a hawk.'

The descent is long, like the descent to hell. Finally, one steps into a narrow street, with folded wings and the memory of the flight.

Opposite the cathedral are the remains of a royal palace resting on powerful Gallo-Roman walls. The palace was often visited by the monarchs of the first two dynasties, until their tastes changed and they moved to Compiègne and Fontainebleau. Stone upon stone like geological strata: the remains of a Roman column, traces of Merovingian buildings, Romanesque and Gothic arches.

Nearby is the Musée de la Vénerie (the Hunting Museum), which the guide praises as unique in Europe. In fact, it is a miserable store of trumpets, horns, stuffed game, hoofs nailed to wooden boards with ribbons of skin, along with portraits of princes, viscounts and dogs. All carefully arranged to give the impression of a complete knowledge of hunting like a sequence of drawings depicting various falls from a horse — on the head, on the back, etcetera — or different stages of deer hunting. I learned that the beautiful word *halali* simply means dispatching a wounded animal. Further on there is a museum of archeology and sculpture in a charming mansion, to which you descend along winding lanes.

The Halatte Forest in the vicinity was a kind of holy health resort in Roman times. Stone people on votive offerings raise their stone shirts to expose their pudenda. I do not know if these bas-reliefs have been scrutinized by men of science; surely they present a prominent source of medical research. In the Dijon stone collection there are stone lungs presented to the gods by some ancient tubercular. At first the sculpted heads appear as the heads of the healed. One must stoop and take a closer look. Yes. They are the faces of idiots, melancholics — the malady which the sculptor (a stonemason rather than an artist) defined with a psychiatrist's touch.

On the second floor of the museum, our attention is drawn by a monumental Gothic sculpture of an 'Idiot'. It probably came from the cathedral, occupying a place close to the reptiles on the ladder of Creation. He is not a madman, rather a gentle half-wit, the town fool who wears a red cap and squawks like a cock. His eyes are empty egg-shells, his lips open in an apologetic smile. Beside him rests 'The Head of a Prophet', a masterpiece of early Gothic sculpture, a study in noble wisdom and human dignity; a witness to the Gothic sculptors' scale of humanity.

I pocket both notebook and sketch-pad. It's time for the most pleasant item on the schedule — loafing around,

wandering aimlessly, a guest of perspective,

looking at exotic workshops and stores: the locksmith's, a travel office, the undertaker's,

staring,

picking up pebbles, and throwing them away,

drinking wine in the darkest spots: *Chez Jean, Petit Vatel,*

meeting people,

smiling at girls,

putting your face to walls to catch their smells,

asking conventional questions to check the well of human benevolence,

viewing people with irony and love,

joining a dice game,

visiting an antique shop and asking the price of an ebony music box,

listening to its melody, then leaving,

studying the menus in the windows of exclusive restaurants and indulging in licentious fantasies: lobster or oysters for starters;

ending up at *Au Bon Coin* whose proprietress is kind, has a weak heart and treats you to a liquor called 'Ricard' which has a terrible aniseed taste and can be swallowed only in deference to the natives,

careful reading of the fête's programme and the list of prizes to be won in tombola for the soldiers, and all the other notices, especially those written by hand.

A shadow travels across the sun-dial. In the thick autumn air Senlis sleeps like a pond under a coat of duckweed.

One must move on. Walking towards the station one passes the old churches of Saint-Pierre and Saint-Frambourg dating from the turn of the eleventh and twelfth centuries. Now they are closed. The former contains a super-market, the latter a garage. The French are a rich nation.

Chaâlis

> This old, lonely dwelling of the emperors presents nothing extraordinary besides the ruins of a monastery with Byzantine arcades whose last row is reflected in the mirror of ponds . . .
>
> *Sylvie*

One can travel to Chaâlis by a ramshackle bus from the Senlis station near the war memorial, a hideous masterpiece. On this road rattled the carriage carrying Gérard de Nerval and Sylvie's brother to the last performance in which the poet would see Adrienne, disguised as an angel.

In the literary geography of French Romanticism, the position of Valois corresponds to that of Scotland for the English. It is to Valois that Gérard de Nerval devoted his *Sylvie* written two years before his death when the lights of his Orient were dimming. The writer entered a time of despair as the circle of his travels narrowed to the environs of Paris — small, forsaken towns, hamlets as poor as pigeon-houses, where behind green shutters framed with a rose bush and vine a warbler's cage gently swung. Nothing can be more soothing than a night 'Under the Image of St John' in a room with ancient upholstery and pier-glass. In the evenings girls in white garlands sang in the meadow and bannered boats carried the young to Cythera. In the humid forests of Valois among the cloistered ruins and castles, 'Werther without pistols' hunted chimeras.

Painters and Romantic poets loudly praised the abbey's ruins. It is a pity that so little has survived, since the Chaâlis church was one of the first Cistercian Gothic buildings. Its size was impressive, eighty-one metres by twenty-seven, with both wings of the grand transept ending in five radial chapels. The stems of the columns remain with their capitals as clear as musical notes. The abbey is like a deserted nest under the sky's high vault. Liberated from the stone weight the strong arches, buttresses and pilasters resist the pressure of infinity.

To the immediate left stands a fifteenth-century palace built by Jean Aubert, architect of the Chantilly stables. Inside, the Jacquemart-André collection. A family of great artistic merit whose Parisian mansion on Boulevard Haussmann held their main collection (now a splendid museum). A painter with aristocratic connections told me about a dinner party at the private residence at which the matriarch reproached her husband for keeping 'this terrible Titian' in the dining-room.

The Chaâlis collection cannot match its Parisian rival. It is typical bric-à-brac, charming, yet slightly annoying: an ancient eighteenth-century bust, Dutch still-lives heavy like cooking odours, a copy of the Great Mogul's throne and a Giotto. I disliked the Giotto at first sight. Two dry, conventional *panneaux* in dimmed colour. I confessed my doubts to a museum guard in a navy-blue uniform with silver buttons. He stood near the wall as one expects: half-object, half-human. He slowly lifted his serpent's lids, listened to my complaints and then hissed that the Musée Jacquemart-André held no forgeries. It never had, it does not, nor will it ever contain counterfeits. I left him at the wall. When he withers completely, he will be replaced by a pole-axe or a chair.

Two small rooms on the second floor display Jean-Jacques Rousseau memorabilia. A few imaginary portraits, one depicting a youth sleeping on a park bench ('*J.J. sans argent, sans asile, à Lyon et pourtant sans souci sur l'avenir, passé souvent la nuit à la belle étoile,*' reads the note). A dirty collar in the showcase gives unfavourable evidence of his lady companion, so hated by biographers. We see a hat, a pen and the arm-chair in which the author of *The Confessions* expired. The arm-chair is conjectural. But since no counter-claimant has emerged, it is justly an object of veneration. On the wall an engraving portrays Rousseau's last moments with the alleged last words of the philosopher praising greenery, nature, light and God, and his longing for eternal peace. The aria is long, phoney and operatic.

The environs have romantic, exaggerated names: the Sea of Sand or the Desert. The sea is less than a kilometre in diameter. It looks like the scorched trace of a meteor. The forest is beautiful, thick with birch, oak, and ash, with a copper undergrowth. It is the wild patch of Ermenonville Park. An asphalt road dissects the green. Cars stream without abatement. I am the sole pedestrian. Some cars slow down: they stare.

Ermenonville

French literature was perfectly indifferent to the sight of green. It was Rousseau who revealed it to us. Thus, one can describe him with one word: Rousseau was the first to introduce 'greeness' into our literature.

SAINTE-BEUVE

I continued the recitation of the fragments of *Héloïse* when Sylvie gathered wild strawberries.

Sylvie

The theory of gardens is more indispensable to an understanding of Classicism and pre-Romanticism that the theory of poetry. A walk in Ermenonville is more instructive than reading Delille. The eighteenth-century *jardin paysager* or 'English garden' is a book of poetics, a catalogue of figures and tropes defined by a cascade, a bridge, a cluster of trees, an artificial ruin. Everything needed by tender hearts: 'the grotto of secret meetings', 'the bench of a fatigued mother', 'the tomb of an unhappy lover'. History was ruthless to these sentimental seedlings. Hence the necessity to see Ermenonville, one of the best preserved eighteenth-century gardens.

It was the creation of the Marquis René de Girardin, in Greuze's portrait a homely, pale-faced gentleman with the soft eyes of a hound. Dressed *'avec une élégance naturelle et très aristocratique'* in a Werther costume: a woollen frock-coat, a fancy foulard and leather trousers gartered under the knees. He began his career under the sign of Mars, in deference to family tradition rather than choice. He was a captain at the court of Stanisław Leszczyński, Prince of Lorraine. After the Prince's death, he spent most of his life tending to his inherited estate, and specially to establishing a park on the surrounding wasteland. His book *De la composition des paysages sur le terrain ou Des moyens d'embellir la nature près des habitations, en joignant l'agréable à l'utile* (1777) joins his experience to the soaring spirit of Jean-Jacques Rousseau. Girardin adored the author of *La Nouvelle Héloïse* whose pages are heard in the leaves of Ermenonville. The Marquis based his children's education on *Emile*, enriched with his own inventions. He placed a lunch-basket at the top of a high pole and made his offspring fetch their reward. The children grew up to be normal, however, and even rose to high positions.

The Marquis liked to travel; in his youth he visited Germany, Italy and England, where he was deeply affected by the period's horticultural epidemic. William Kent designed a palace park whose pattern was frequently imitated. The famous dandy Cobham sank a fortune into similar endeavours; and William Shenstone's garden of cascades, ruins and rocks greatly influenced Girardin's aesthetics.

These undertakings coincided with the literary revival of Hesiod, Theocritus and Virgil and the emergence of their followers: Thomson, Gessner, Young, Gray. The patron of French bucolic poetry is old Fénelon. 'The Xanthe River winds among poplars and willows whose fresh, delicate green covers innumerable nests of birds singing day and night. The plains are covered by golden corn; hills sag under the weight of the vine and the rising galleries of fruit trees. Here nature was joyful and attractive, and the sky was sweet and clear. The earth was ready to issue from her bosom new riches in return for human toil.'

Sentimental landscape is the scenery of sentimental economy; the springs of utopian socialism streamed in Arcadia. Virgil walks with Proudhon. The peasant woman Proxionë 'prepared wonderful cakes. She bred bees whose honey was sweeter than nectar which dripped down the oak timbers in the Golden Age. Cows came of their own accord to offer torrents of milk . . . daughters imitated their mothers singing with great pleasure as the sheep were lead to the meadows. To this tender tune lambs danced on the grass.'

In addition to the areas devoted to philosophical meditation and the higher emotions of the Marquis and his guests, a portion of the park was given to 'our dearest peasants'. Here the art of archery (highly venerated in Valois from time immemorial) was practised; and the country musicians' rondo under an oak sparked the traditional *guillot, saute, perrette*.

Des habitants de l'heureuse Arcadie,
Si vous avez les nobles moeurs,
Restez ici, goûtez-y les douceurs
Et les plaisirs d'une innocente vie . . .

The Marquis ordered this to be cut in stone because he was also a poet, and the fact that Ermenonville Park is full of his poems indicates that he cherished certain illusions regarding his talents.

Out-door concerts for the upper class were often held on Poplar Island. Girardin met the author of *The Country Prophet* through their mutual musical interests. On 20 May 1778, Jean-Jacques arrived at Ermenonville and settled into a park pavilion with the ever-present Thérèse Levasseur. These were the philosopher's last days. He wandered in the neighbourhood ('my mind needs movement'), his pockets full of bird-seed. He played with the children and told them fairy-tales. He considered writing a sequel to *Emile* and conjured musical ideas. Primarily, he walked in the park as became the author of *Reveries of the Solitary Walker*, enraptured by his beloved plant — the woodruff. 'These six weeks were absent from the history of Rousseau's writing; not a single line of his work bears an Ermenonville date.' He lived in the Marquis's park as in the heart of a dream realized.

Through the mercy of nature his death was easy, though its suddenness bred suspicion. On the night of 4 July 1778, his body was lowered by torchlight to a tomb on Poplar Island, the most beautiful area of Ermenonville Park. The inscription on the sepulchre reads: '*Ici repose l'homme de la Nature et de la Vérité*'. The funeral's romantic nature was counterpointed by the clergy's refusal to bury Voltaire, whose death occurred five weeks earlier.

The body of Rousseau rested in a vault decorated with his bas-relief portrait by Lesueur. In accordance with a decree of the Convention (and through no small effort of Thérèse Levasseur) his remains were transferred to the Panthéon. But the spirit of Jean-Jacques lingered in Ermenonville, which became the site of literary, philosophical, even imperial pilgrimages. It is the traditional setting of Napoleon's famous remark: '*L'avenir dira s'il n'eût pas mieux valu pour le repos de la terre, que ni Rousseau ni moi n'eussions existé.*'

The air of the park is green and sultry from expired sentiments. The paths are for those without aim, only to wander along bridges suspended over artificial waters toward the Altar to Dreams. Today, no one rests his hot forehead upon it. The Temple of Philosophy (devoted to Montaigne and deliberately unfinished) evokes no deeper reflections than to discourage man-made ruins; history excels in this production. Some columns have separated from the temple. Patient roots press them deeper and deeper into the ground.

Rousseau's tomb is not the sole stone which bespeaks the passing of time. On the high, left bank of the river Aunette, rests 'the Unknown Tomb'. In the summer of 1791, a thirty-year-old neurasthenic committed a picturesque suicide. The '*vicitme de l'amour*', as he called himself in his note to Marquis de Girardin, asked to be buried '*sous quelque épais feuillage*'.

Near the cascade lies the Grotto of the Naiads. From a bench Marie-Antoinette gazed at the philosopher's sepulchre reflected in the still waters. The noble-sized, rectangular stone greys in the long grass. The poplars are tall. In the wind the dry, green flames look like Tintoretto's angels.

Ermenonville, a subtle instrument of sentiment and reflection, has been severely damaged by time. Numerous buildings have disappeared: the Altar to Friendship, the Obelisk of the Pastoral Muse, and the Pyramid, a homage to bucolic poets from Theocritus to Gessner.

The park is now the property of a Touring Club. Excursions are herded along described paths. Rousseau's tomb — *et voilà*. The cascade — *tiens, tiens, tiens*. The Altar to Dreams — *c'est à droit*. The air is laden with moisture and sighs: Marquis de Girardin's spirit covers his eyes and weeps. One must visit Ermenonville in early spring or late autumn when the Naiads are asleep, the cascade is silent and the drained lake around Poplar Island appears as a mirror of mud.

The Return

The charms of the countryside — no sense of symmetry, of time, and an aversion to stupid rules.

One needs cunning to learn where the Ermenonville-Paris bus stops. '*On ne sait jamais,*' sometimes at the bridge, other times at the *tabac*. I stake it on the *tabac* and win. We enter the night.

A stopover in Senlis. At the stop a soldier and girl embrace tightly, lost in each other. The driver coughs, blows the horn, flashes the lights, then turns to the passengers and smiles. Finally, he starts the bus slowly so that the soldier can leave her without undue haste and jump in at the corner. On the radio Edith Piaf complains:

La fille de joie est belle
Au coin de la rue là-bas
Elle a une clientèle
Qui lui remplit son bas

When I return in twenty-five years' time, Piaf will be a dead star like

Mistinguette. Her name will be a link with my generation, those who survived the same wars. I shall be understood whenever I casually mention her name.

After twenty-five years, how many generations of carp will have bitten the slime of the pond near the palace of Chantilly. Only Sassetta will be the same, and the virtue of poverty flying to the heavens like a stilled Eleatic arrow. Thanks to Sassetta I shall step into the same river, and time, the 'boy playing with stones', will be merciful for a moment.

On the move again. I rush towards death. In my eyes — Paris — the chatter of lights.